RED MAGNOLIA

NIGHTGARDEN SAGA BOOK #1

LUCY HOLDEN

FEHU PRESS

For the gorgeous girls from Yandi, who listened to me talk about the Nightgarden Saga whilst knee deep in Pilbara dirt.

PROLOGUE

DEEPWATER HOLLOW

*D*ear Tessa,
     It's a year today since I watched you die. If one more person tells me not to feel guilty, I might actually lose it. As long as we were still the Ellory twins, somehow it didn't seem so bad that it was just us and Connor. But me alone is different.

Alone, I am an orphan.

I never felt like one before, though technically I guess we both were after Mom died.

Connor misses you. He doesn't say much, but I can tell. He's my legal guardian now, which is actually just weird, since he's barely twenty-one. Someone had to do the job, I guess. We changed his name to Ellory before we moved. We both know his dad is never coming back. And although he never said anything, I know he hated having to explain who he was to teachers or doctors, every time there was a legal form to sign.

There've been way too many forms, lately.

I'm starting a new school today. I couldn't face going back to the old one after you died. I did homeschooling for the rest of the school year, and we moved over the summer. Connor made me go to that camp you and I applied to for two weeks, I think just to get me out of the house while he packed up your things. I sure couldn't face doing it. I didn't tell anyone at camp you were dead, just that you changed your mind about coming. It seemed easier. I actually talked about you the whole time as if you were still alive, which is pretty messed up, I know, but a whole lot easier than telling people your twin sister died. Nobody knows what to say to that, including me.

I know I should have written all this earlier. But today is the first day I've felt like I can talk to you directly. Or write, at least. I can't stand the idea of "journaling," as the grief therapist called it. It feels self-indulgent and pretentious. But writing to you is easy. You always knew what I thought before I ever said it anyway.

My new school is in Deepwater Hollow, Mississippi. It's a little town an hour or so upriver from Baton Rouge, no more than a dot on the map. I'm glad to be leaving the city. To be leaving Louisiana. Everything about our old place reminded me of you.

I want Connor to feel good about this. There are more old plantation ruins here than anywhere else in the continental US, and plenty of grants to restore them, apparently. We used Mom's insurance money to buy a huge, decaying antebellum house on the Mississippi after Connor designed a winning proposal for it. If he makes good on his plans, and I know he will, he'll be able to bid for more. He says it's a new beginning for us. I want to believe that, even if the ruins of the past are a strange place to look for a new beginning.

This place is insane, truly. You would love it. Big, old oaks hung with Spanish moss hide the house from the road, and down back a little wood dock juts out onto the river. The red magnolia trees you loved so much grow by the porch and run the length of the back lawn. Their scent reminds me of you.

Plaster is crumbling from the ceiling, and we're using kerosene lanterns and an icebox until Connor fixes the wiring. It feels as if Miss Haversham might live in the attic, though so far, it's just been the bugs and us.

I'm writing this from the school parking lot on the first day of senior year. I'm still driving the old pink Mustang convertible you and I bought together. When the crystal you put on the rearview mirror catches the light, the turquoise in it reminds me of your eyes. Which is weird when you think about it, because actually, I see your eyes every time I look into a mirror. But that's the thing about being an identical twin. Almost everything about us looks the same, but no matter how hard I try, I can't make my eyes look like yours. Some days I stare into the mirror at them until I ache, just hoping I catch a glimpse of you inside them.

Because I miss you, Tessa. And the truth is, missing you is the reason I haven't written. Because if I let myself think about how much I miss you, everything in me starts to crumble, and I think that if I let even one piece fall, the whole of me will come tumbling down in a way even Connor's DIY cannot fix.

A new school might not be able to bring you back. But maybe, if I try hard enough, it might bring me back.

The bell is ringing. I have to go.

Wish me luck.

Your twin,

Harper

CHAPTER 1

CURSED

*D*eepwater High has fewer faces in the entire student body than the senior-year class at my old school, but I'm pretty sure every single one of them is staring at me in the corridor. I was expecting the usual first day once-over, but this feels next-level, and by the time I clear the registrar and find my new English class, I'm starting to miss Baton Rouge. Everyone else is seated already.

"Ah," says Mr. Corbin, making a mock bow. "Miss Ellory. The new tenant of Deepwater's favorite Gothic mansion graces us with her presence." I have to do the awkward, newbie walk of shame through another barrage of curious eyes, to a desk crammed between a tall, pale boy with floppy brown hair falling over his face, and a dark-haired girl who has her head down writing notes. I slide into my seat, face burning.

"Mr. Marigny," Mr. Corbin addresses the pale boy, who looks up warily. "Perhaps you could show your new neighbor where we are in the textbook." He turns back to the board. The boy leans across the aisle and flips my book open.

"There," he says, pointing to the page. He doesn't look at me when he speaks. When he turns back to his book, I see the flush rising on his neck, and I realize he's not rude, just shy. I know how he feels. I glance at his paper and see his name at the top: Jeremiah Marigny.

I can almost hear Tessa beside me, giggling at the name. Our mom loved old rock songs, and when we were kids she'd play one song on loop whenever we were driving around. There's a line in it that goes around in my head: *Jeremiah was a bullfrog.* I write it on the side of my page, making swirling patterns out of the letters, getting lost in the finer points so Mr. Corbin's voice fades away. The words become a vine down the margin of my book. The vine becomes the frame for a window. I sketch the wood dock at the back of our new home as if I were sitting inside the window looking out and then add a full moon blazing down. I'm so lost in my drawing that I'm startled when the clatter of chairs signals the end of class. I scramble for my bag and realize, too late, that Jeremiah has seen the words in the margin. Even made into a vine, they are unmistakable. His eyes meet mine, wide and dark and deep somehow, as if he already knows how much the world is going to hurt him.

"I'm sorry," I mutter. It's all I can think of. He tilts his head and shrugs, almost smiling, then slings his bag over his shoulder and is gone. For a lanky boy, he moves fast. He's out of the room before I've even stood up.

"Don't worry about Jeremiah," says the girl who was sitting on the other side of me. "He's shy, is all." Her skin is tawny in the morning sun, eyes dark over slanted cheekbones. She's so beautiful it's like standing in a gallery just looking at her. My fingers itch to sketch her face. "I'm Avery."

"Hey, Avery." I gesture at the offending words on the page before me. "I didn't mean anything by it. It's just the name, you know? I couldn't help but think of the song."

"Like I said, don't worry." She gives me a friendly smile that I could literally hug her for about now. "We've been ragging on Jeremiah about that name since grade school. He won't mind." She glances at my class schedule and map. "I can walk you to the art hall if you like. My class isn't far away."

"Thank you," I say gratefully. Map reading has never been my strong point. We head out along the breezeway, and I try to ignore all the curious stares. "So Mr. Corbin mentioned that Jeremiah is our neighbor," I say, more to make conversation than anything else. "I hadn't noticed anyone living nearby."

"He's not your neighbor anymore. I'm not sure that he ever really was." There's something in the way she says it that makes me look sideways at her. "The house you bought is the Marigny mansion. It belonged to his family."

It takes me a moment to digest that. Connor handled the documents for the house. I never looked hard at the names involved. Besides, the mansion is so decayed it hadn't occurred to me that anyone could have tried to actually live in it in recent years. Connor worked all summer while I was away at camp just to make it safe to step inside.

"You mean he used to live there?" I imagine a lifetime amid the crumbling plaster, lack of electricity, and rusted bathtub, and think it's no wonder Jeremiah looks so sad.

"Not exactly. He and his parents lived in a trailer. They parked on the grounds there, sometimes." Avery chews her lip, clearly holding back.

Normally I'd be far too shy to ask further. But my natural introversion is overpowered by the memory of Jeremiah's hurt eyes and the fear that I'll inadvertently do or say something else hurtful.

"Um, Avery?" We're nearly across the sloping lawn to the art hall. "If there's some kind of story about our house, it would really help to know about it so I don't do anything else stupid that might upset someone."

Avery shrugs. "It's nothing, really. All the old places around here have a story, you know?" Her eyes slide away.

"So, what's the story with mine?"

She gives me a look like she'd rather not say but knows I won't let it go. "Your house has been in the Marigny family for as long as anyone can remember, but it's been a ruin for decades now, and even longer since anyone actually lived in it." She looks around as if to make sure nobody is in earshot, then leans in and lowers her voice.

"Thing is, a few months ago Jeremiah's parents both died in a car crash. It was awful. My aunt is a nurse at the hospital, and she said the bodies were so messed up you could barely recognize them. Jeremiah doesn't have any brothers or sisters, and his parents never had a lot of money. The sale of the Marigny mansion is all the money he was left with."

I feel humiliation crawl up my spine like a roly-poly bug. "So I just made fun of the boy with dead parents whose house I stole."

She stares at me a moment and then bursts out laughing. "Well," she says, "when you put it like that, I guess."

"At least that explains why everyone is looking at me. Thanks for telling me, Avery." I give her a smile and turn toward the art hall.

"Harper, wait." When I turn back, she's shifting her feet, like she's trying to decide whether to speak or not. "You should know. It's not just the car crash or dead parents that's the story with the Marigny mansion."

"Then what is?"

She tilts her head awkwardly and does her feet-shifting thing again. "You know that Deepwater is real old country, right? Like, that mansion you bought—it's so old, nobody around here even knows the truth about it anymore."

"Sure." I look at her, waiting.

"So, the story is just something everyone hears, you know, growing up. They say that something bad happened there, a long time ago. People died. And that afterwards, there was a curse put on the house, like an old voodoo thing."

My eyes bug a little. "An old voodoo thing? Seriously?"

She nods. "The story went that so long as the Marigny mansion stayed in the family, the curse would be contained, and nobody else would die. But if it was sold . . ." her voice trails off and she gives me an apologetic shrug.

"Oh, great." I try to keep a flippant tone, but I'd be lying if I said my heart didn't stop a little at that. I've had about enough of death to last me forever. "Well, I guess every old place around here has a story, like you said."

"Maybe."

I don't really want to hear any more stories, but we've come this far, and there's something in her voice that says she isn't quite done. "Go on, then. Give me the rest." Avery meets my eyes, and now there is no hint of laughter in her face.

"It wasn't Jeremiah who chose to sell the house. It was his parents. They were real happy about it, too. The night they signed the papers, they went to the local roadhouse. Bought a round for the whole bar. They told everyone they were putting a down payment on a place down in Biloxi. Time to leave the past behind, they said, and move on."

I feel a cold sensation in my spine.

"They never even made it home." Avery's words drop into the day like the first cold touch of winter. "They left the roadhouse and crashed the car, not a mile up the road. It happened the very same day they signed the Marigny mansion over to your family. That's it, Harper. That's the story. That's why everyone is looking at you. They think you're living in a cursed house, and they're all wondering what happens next."

CHAPTER 2

VEILS

*I*t's a relief to go into the quiet art hall. The teacher has a sweet face and a funky, bohemian look, and she thankfully doesn't remark on my newbie status. "I'm Miss Calhoun," she says in a low voice, steering me past the other students toward an easel. "We're working on a layering technique that will be the background for a new piece. Choose a watercolor and apply it in layers, like veils." She demonstrates then gives me a once-over. "You might want to tie that hair up." I flush and scrabble through my bag for a hair tie. Tessa and I had the same copper hair, so thick and curly Mom gave up trying to tame it when we were kids and just let it grow. It's been down to my waist for as long as I can remember. I wrap it up in a big knot and pull the hair tie around it. I know it makes me look like I'm the beehive queen, but I'm already embarrassed enough, and I figure there isn't any point trying to pretend to an elegance I definitely don't possess. Mom always said our hair and coloring were a gift from a distant ancestor. Maybe if we lived in Europe, she'd be right, but I feel like ivory skin and deep copper ringlets aren't much of an advantage in southern Mississippi.

I get to work, welcoming the soothing strokes of my paintbrush and the dreamy music she has going in the background. There are only a few of us in the class. One of them is Jeremiah. I glance at him once, but he seems immersed in his painting and doesn't look at me.

My brush rolls over the page and gradually the layers form the same scene I sketched earlier, with a ghostly moon reflecting in the water. I like the way the veils make the image emerge, as if the scene creates itself, rather than me painting it. I'm surprised when the class comes to an end. Miss Calhoun stands behind me as I pack up.

"I know that view," she says, smiling. "Looking out over the river from behind the Marigny place." As soon as she speaks, she goes red and glances at Jeremiah, but he is already out the door, walking up over the hill. "Oh, dear," she sighs. "That was clumsy of me."

"Don't worry." I can feel the curious eyes of the rest of the class on me. "At least you aren't the one living in it."

"Oh!" Miss Calhoun waves a hand in a not-entirely-reassuring effort at dismissal. "Never mind those old stories."

I give her what I hope seems like a convincing smile. "I'm more worried about whether or not my stepbrother Connor will actually make the water tap work, to be honest." That at least gets a rumble of laughter.

At lunch I sit with Avery and her friends and try to remember their names. Jeremiah Marigny, I notice, is sitting on his own at a table a little distant from ours.

"Should we ask him to eat with us?" I ask Avery under cover of conversation.

"You could try," she says, equally quietly. "But Jeremiah isn't really one for chat, especially now, since his parents died."

I know how that feels. It hadn't mattered so much after Mom died. There was Tessa and me, and because we were our own little friendship bubble, people weren't scared to talk to us. And Tessa was always bubbly. People were drawn to her. Mom used to say that Tessa did the talking for us both, while I did the listening. I know she said it because she worried I felt overshadowed by Tessa, but the truth is, I never did. I could easily listen to her chatter on all day and never get bored. It was only after she died that I realized I didn't really know how to talk at all—and by then, nobody knew how to talk to me either. In the end, it was easier to be homeschooled and communicate in monosyllabic peace with Connor.

The rest of the day passes in a blur of faces, names, and embarrassing class entrances. When the final bell rings, I spot Jeremiah leaving the building and walk faster to catch up to him. He's really tall and moves so fast I almost have to run. "Hey," I say, puffing slightly as we near the parking lot. "Jeremiah. I just wanted to say I'm really sorry for making fun of your name this morning." I smile, but he doesn't look at me, and it might be my imagination, but he seems to have upped his pace even more. He's looking uneasily toward the parking lot, like he's expecting someone. "I wasn't actually making fun of it," I say. "I draw a lot."

"I know." He stops and turns to face me. "I saw you in art hall."

"I didn't realize it was your house we bought." He's looking at something over my shoulder and couldn't be less welcoming, but I plow on regardless. "Or about your parents." This is awkward as hell, but if anyone has experience in awkward, dead-family conversations, it's me, so I push on. "My parents are both dead, too." I can't quite bring myself to mention Tessa. "So, I guess I just wanted to say that I'm sorry."

He nods but still doesn't smile.

"Anyway." I'm definitely embarrassed now. "I just wanted to say that." I start walking away, feeling like a prize idiot, when he takes my arm and stops me. His face is pained, as if he's already regretting his decision to talk to me. "If you really are sorry about the house," he says, "maybe you could ask your brother to sell it back to me."

"Sell it back to you?" I stare at him. "Why? And it's my name on the deed, not Connor's."

His eyes widen. "You own it?"

I nod. "My brother has power of attorney because I'm underage, but it's in my name. Connor won a grant to renovate it. I'm really sorry, Jeremiah. I know it must mean a lot to you, but I can't just sell it back."

"No. You don't understand." If his agitation wasn't already clear enough, he grips my arm hard enough to hurt. "You need to sell that house, Harper. It isn't safe there, for you or your brother." He looks over my shoulder again and his face tightens, like he's afraid.

"Ow, Jeremiah. You're hurting me." I pull my arm away and look around. There's an old teal-colored Chevy truck pulling into the lot, the kind guys always say they want to buy and restore but never do. I can't see who's driving it, but Jeremiah is watching it like it's coming for him. I lower my voice. "Avery told me the story about the house, but surely you don't believe it's actually cursed?" I feel stupid even saying the word.

He laughs, but not in amusement. It's more the kind of laugh someone makes when they know something you don't, a little wild and out of control. I don't like how tense he is, and I step aside as he pushes past me toward the Chevy. "You don't know anything about the curse," he says, and now he just sounds tired, almost despairing. "Please, Harper. I've already sent a lawyer's letter to the house. It should be there when you get home today. At least look at it and consider the offer."

"Ok," I say. "I'll look. But I have to tell you, Jeremiah—even if I wanted to sell the house, I don't think my brother would be very happy giving up a grant he worked all summer to get. I'm sorry, truly I am, especially about your parents. I just can't see that selling you back the house is going to help anything."

He's already walking toward the lot and doesn't answer. There's a man leaning against the grill of the Chevy, arms folded, watching us. He looks Connor's age, maybe a little older, early twenties. He's wearing faded jeans that look like he was born in them and a V-neck a shade darker than his truck. He's taller even than Jeremiah, but lean and hard rather than lanky, and outdoor-adventure tanned. There's a three-day stubble on his face that looks like it's a way of life rather than an accident. His tousled dark hair has nothing to do with product, and his features seem carved from polished wood, unyielding and timeless. Then his eyes hit mine, and despite the distance between us, they are as clear as if he stood right in front of me.

They're an intense slate color, like dark thunderheads rolling in over the water. But it's the way they're looking at me, rather than their startling depth, that stops me right in my tracks. He is unnervingly still, his face unsmiling. Even from across the lot, hostility comes at me, as if the tropical storm in his eyes is about to make landfall.

Jeremiah opens the door of the truck and glances back, his eyes shifting between the man and me, and I realize it wasn't dislike I saw on his face earlier.

It was fear.

The man's eyes shift away from me and I feel them go, as if an invisible cord is released. I must have glanced away for a moment, because when I look back, the Chevy is already reversing.

Jeremiah glances at me through the window, and I can't tell if he is more angry or afraid. The Chevy pulls out and I watch it go, feeling even more disturbed than I did when Avery first told me about the curse on my house.

CHAPTER 3

MANSION

"So that's the relative who's taking care of Jeremiah." Avery's car is parked next to mine, and she's watching the teal Chevy pull out of the lot with almost as much interest as I am.

"His name is Antoine Marigny." The girl with Avery has skin like liquid caramel and a mass of braids wound into a roll almost as huge as my own. Her name is Cass, I remember. She sat with us at lunch. "He's a cousin or something who's come to stay with Jeremiah after the accident." She shoots Avery a wicked grin. "Let's hope he decides to make the move permanent." They both crack up, and I try to laugh with them, because trying to explain what just happened is impossible, and anyway, by the time I'm unlocking my car I'm sure I must have mistaken the way he looked at me.

"Hey, Harper." Cass is smiling. She was nice at lunch, I remember, chatting away without the hidden little barbs that some of the other girls threw into the conversation just to let me know I was in their territory and shouldn't forget my place. "There's a party out at the old place at Perdu Inlet this weekend. You should come."

"Thanks." I return her smile. "I'll have to ask my brother, but that sounds great." I go to get in my car and pause. "You guys have known Jeremiah since grade school, right?" They nod. "I was just wondering what he's normally like," I say, trying to sound casual. "I know he's just lost his parents, but he seemed a bit—well, strange, I guess."

"Jeremiah's fine. The Marignys have always had a bit of a name around town, and it's been worse since the accident. Deepwater is one of the oldest towns in Mississippi." Avery shrugs. "There are lots of old prejudices, you know?"

"Like what?" I say, looking between them. Avery and Cass exchange a knowing look.

"Well, you might have noticed Cass and I aren't exactly traditional southern belle material." I maintain a neutral expression, not really too sure what to say to that. "Cass's family leads back to chains," Avery says bluntly.

Cass grins at my shock. "And Avery's family were Natchez. They called this land home before white folks ever turned up."

"If you ever want to watch a teacher squirm," says Avery conspiratorially, "watch Cass and I bring up our family histories. Guaranteed to make a classroom silent in seconds. We're like walking evidence of the bad, old days nobody likes to admit to."

"Wow." I look between them. "Respect."

"So, I guess we have that in common. The bit where nobody knows what to say." Cass tilts her head to the side. "Well, except for the cursed house, and, you know." She breaks off awkwardly.

"The dead parents?" I finish for her. "Yeah. We could take everyone as the best conversation stoppers." I leave Tessa out again. I do it so often now I barely notice. "Thanks, guys," I say, and I mean it. "Today really would have sucked without you."

"Cool cool," says Avery. I've heard her do that twice today, like the two words are actually one, but dropping the *l* each time, so it sounds like *coocoo*. They both smile and get into Avery's car. "And about Jeremiah," Avery says as I open my car door. "Don't mind him, really. He's a nice guy. He's just having a really hard time."

I nod. "Sure." But as they turn toward town and I take the route out along the river that takes me home, I wonder if they're talking about the same Jeremiah I am. Because something tells me there is more truth to whatever old-town stories are told about the Marigny family than people might think.

Connor's pickup is out front when I get home, which is strange since he's been working really long days all summer. The door is open, but that's not surprising. It's so huge and heavy, it doesn't actually close properly, so we leave it wide open most days. It isn't like there's anything to steal anyway. Most of our stuff is still in storage in Baton Rouge. Connor is sitting in the kitchen at the old wooden table that we picked up at a garage sale our first week here. He's reading something with his back to me. My heart sinks a little. I'm pretty sure I know what it is.

"How was your first day?" He asks without turning around.

"It was fine. I played nice with others." I drop my bag by the door and take a seat across from him. Connor has olive skin to my ivory, dark hair to my copper, and blue eyes that are steady and clear. He's generally pretty quiet, especially since Tessa died, but today he seems even more reserved than normal. "Let me guess," I say, nodding at the paper in his hand. "An offer to buy the house?"

"Yeah. And not just an offer." He hands it to me, and my eyes widen at the sum on it. "How did you know?"

"I met Jeremiah Marigny at school today. He said his lawyers had sent an offer, but I didn't realize it would be so big."

"It's almost half as much again as we paid for it." Connor is frowning. "Where does a kid like Jeremiah Marigny get that kind of money?"

I think of Antoine Marigny's lean, hard body, his eyes staring me down, and a faint shiver ripples my skin. "There's a relative." I hope my voice sounds steadier than I feel. "His name is Antoine, I think. He picked Jeremiah up from school today."

"In a gold-plated Mercedes, I'm guessing, if he's got cash flow like that."

"Not quite. But his truck was an old Chevy, one of those classic ones. And it looked like it had been fully restored, you know? It wasn't ostentatious or anything. Just—careful. There was something about him. I could just kind of tell he had money. He had that look." As I say it, I realize it's true. As casual as his clothes had been, and as much as Antoine had looked like he could as easily be underneath the Chevy fixing it as driving it, there'd been something in the way he held himself that said the world was his to own. "He struck me as the kind of guy who doesn't like things getting in his way."

"Well, regardless of where it came from, this is a solid offer. What do you want to do?" Connor is pulling a beer from the cooler we're using until the wiring is fixed, so I can't see his face. He throws me a soda can without turning around.

"It's not just my decision, Connor." This is uncomfortable territory. "It's your money too."

"Your mom left that money for you and Tessa." His voice roughens slightly on my sister's name, and I realize it's probably the first time I've heard him say it out loud since the day we put her ashes in the ground. I find it suddenly hard to swallow. "This offer would give you enough to go to college, buy an apartment even. It's far more than this place is worth, even restored."

I look around at the decaying plaster, the old chandelier hanging at a crazy angle from a crack in the roof, the grand staircases that look like something Scarlett O'Hara would sweep down in a wide ballgown. "But you love it, don't you," I say to Connor's back. "This restoration is your dream. You worked on the plans for that proposal every spare minute you had for the last year."

I know the Marigny mansion is his dream. I know he'll never get another shot like this at making it come true. And Connor knows, too, because he swallows his beer and looks away when he answers me. "You should take the money."

"Maybe." I look at the paper again. "But I'm going to think on it for a day or so first." The truth is that while restoring the mansion might have begun as Connor's dream, over time it has become mine, too. The new beginning we both want. That we need. Giving up on it feels like one more death in a life that has already seen too many. The mansion represents hope, and if there's one thing that Connor and I are sorely in need of, it's a little hope.

"Harper." He looks at me as if he's considering what to say next.

"There's something else. It's stupid, but I heard it in town today, and you should probably know."

"It's cursed," I cut him off. "This place. The Marigny mansion, as everyone calls it. I heard."

Connor nods. "I guess after everything that's happened, I just thought you'd want to know."

I give him a half smile. "Does it matter? I'm pretty sure we're cursed anyhow." Seeing his brow start to frown in worry, I stand up abruptly and grab my bag. "I've got homework to do," I say, heading for the stairs. "I'll think about it, ok?"

"Ok." I think Connor is as relieved as I am to drop it. We've never been big on confiding our feelings—that was more his and Tessa's thing. Connor and I have comfortable silence down to an art form. "I might head into town and pick up some steaks for dinner. I'll be back before dark."

"Sure." I know that what he really means is that the beer is running low, but I don't comment on his drinking, just like he doesn't comment when I play the same song over and over, because it's the last one I remember listening to with Tessa. It's how we've managed to get through the last year, by silently accepting each other's weirdness. I hadn't really thought about it until now, but I guess that in that sense, Connor and I actually are family, albeit an entirely strange one.

"Hey, Harper." I turn at the top of the stairs. Connor is at the door, hovering uncertainly. "Whatever you decide, I just want you to know it's fine." He pauses, as if unsure of how to say what he wants to. "If you want to move into something on your own," he says finally, "I'll understand."

He doesn't wait for an answer. I hear his truck start up and he's gone. I head up into my room, my head swirling from the day.

CHAPTER 4

RIVER

To my own surprise, I actually love my bedroom in this house. *Mine for now*, I remind myself as I open the door. It's bigger than the entire classroom at school. Connor says it was once a "state room," where important visitors would stay. Since I doubt the governor will visit us any time soon, I figured I could take it. There are four windows along the west wall that face out over the dock and the river beyond. They are all recessed with seats below, and I take turns sitting in each one to study. I leave the French windows wide open all the time. It's a nightmare for bugs, but there's something about the scent of the river on a magnolia breeze that makes me feel like anything is possible. Until we have electricity, I've strung up lines of solar-powered fairy lights over my bed, which is the only amazing piece of furniture in the room. Connor made a huge, four-poster frame and hung it with mosquito net. He says that if I can't have a show-pony bed in a room this size, I never will, and even though I thought it was ridiculous when he was building it, I love it now. It's big enough for a party and I cover it in cushions, so it feels like my very own little cave.

I pull off my jeans and throw on old shorts and a T-shirt that won't suffer from charcoal dust. My easel is set up in one of the alcoves, and

I take out my sketchbook and prop it up. I have a ton of homework to do, but after such a long day and so much drama, all I want to do is sketch. I think about the assignment Miss Calhoun is setting us, and what I might want to put over the layered backdrop of river and moon.

It's still afternoon and dusk is a ways off, but when I look out the window, I can imagine how it will be when night falls and the moon is high on the water. This is the window that I saw through earlier today in class, with vine around it, even though there is none growing there now. I slip back into the sketch and try to imagine the face that stares out from it.

At first, all I can see is Tessa, and I nearly walk away from the easel. I gave up sketching faces for months after she died for this reason. It felt like every time I closed my eyes, I saw Tessa's face on the day she fell away from me, her pale lips, her dull eyes that wouldn't stay open no matter how hard she tried. But I've learned to think through that, mainly because I can hear her calling me a coward. Tonight, I make my mind still until a face starts to appear. My hand moves swiftly on the page with charcoal and the outline emerges. I step back and look at it critically, then realize I'm in the wrong place. I need to be down on the dock looking up at the window, so I can imagine the face staring out.

I take my sketchbook and easel to the wide staircase. Even with rotting floorboards and a stained railing, it's impossible to descend it without feeling like someone should be announcing me. *Ladies and gentlemen—Miss Harper Ellory, accompanied by . . .*

An image of Antoine Marigny's face crosses my mind, making me stop right there in the middle of the staircase.

"Oh, please," I say out loud, pleased to hear that my innate sarcasm is still alive. "Could you be any more of a cliché?" I'm not sure if I'm referring to my fantasy of descending the stairs southern-belle style or the highly disturbing image of Antoine Marigny waiting for me at the bottom of them. He wouldn't be dressed as a gentleman, I think, as I go out the back door and down the tangle that used to be a sloping lawn to the jetty, grabbing the Bluetooth speaker as I go. He'd be the pirate running contraband upriver under cover of darkness, pistol in one hand and whiskey in the other, with ladies waiting at every darkened cove.

I roll my eyes at my own fancy. Tessa used to love it when I did this—imagine someone we'd met as part of a story. It feels lonely to imagine it without her. I push it from my mind and set my easel up on the end of the jetty, facing out over the river. I can look over my shoulder at the house to fix the window in my mind, but I want to watch the light change over the water. In the distance I can hear a motorboat coming downriver. I press play on my painting playlist and say a silent prayer of thanks when the soft piano of Ludovico Einaudi flows out across the river. *Perfect.*

The charcoal moves swiftly, and the afternoon slides away. Insects hang over the slow-moving river, incandescent in the golden sun. The face under my fingers isn't one I recognize, but I keep going, because sometimes what happens under charcoal surprises even me. Gradually the features emerge: wide, almond-shaped eyes above angled cheekbones and set under a high, intelligent brow. Sculpted lips, slightly parted, as if a secret smile lurks just behind them. A choker at the throat with an old-fashioned pendant at the center, touched by spiral tendrils of hair that fall artfully from a smooth coiffure. It's only as I sketch in the elegant nose that I realize the face is neither Caucasian nor Black, nor even Native American, but rather something quite different, angular and wild and impossibly beautiful. It's also a face I've never seen before.

I step back from the easel. The engine in the distance has died. The day is fading into the gloaming and the air is still. *Who are you?* I silently ask the woman on the page. She stares back at me with that knowing smile, and I realize I've sketched in a hand holding back the curtain, as if she's peeking out of the window at a party below. There is something in her eyes that makes me feel cold and uneasy. I turn, half expecting to find her lurking in the house behind me, but the windows are dark and empty.

I turn back to find a boat drifting right in front of me. Standing in the cockpit, hair tousled and arms burnished from the sun, is Antoine

Marigny, in a loose cotton shirt and faded shorts, looking uncannily like the pirate I'd imagined earlier. He leaps barefoot out of the still-moving boat onto the jetty in one fluid movement and ties it in a deft twist of rope.

"Hey." I'm too startled to say anything else.

"Hey." He's smiling, and I'm just thinking I might have misjudged him on first impressions when he catches sight of the sketch on my easel, and the smile disappears. "Did you draw that?" He stares at the sketch as if he's seen a ghost. I nod. The dying sun finds a golden reflection in his slate eyes, making them glitter with a hard light. He gestures at the sketch. "Where's the original?"

I frown. "There isn't one. I sketched it."

"You didn't just come up with that face," he says bluntly. "You must have copied it from something."

"Well, I didn't." I'm starting to feel indignant. "And since you've shown up here without so much as a phone call, maybe you should try introducing yourself before commenting on my work." I hold out my hand. "I'm Harper Ellory."

He glances at my hand but doesn't take it. "I know who you are." Any trace of his initial smile is long gone. "My nephew sent you some papers to sign."

"And you're Antoine Marigny. I saw you at school today, picking up Jeremiah." I'm pleased to hear my voice is steady. "But if you've come for the papers, I haven't signed them yet."

"Why not?" He folds his arms and leans against the post.

"Because I'm not sure I want to sell the house."

He tilts his head. "I could always make you," he says softly.

"Oh?" I fold my own arms. "And how, exactly, would you go about that?"

His eyes lock on mine, holding them with an unsettling intensity. "You should sign the papers."

"Really?" I raise my eyebrows. "Does that usually work for you? Turning up at a stranger's house at dusk and just ordering them to do what you want?"

His eyes narrow. "Yes, actually," he says slowly. "As a general rule, it does."

We stare at each other for a moment. I feel an odd sensation, as if the air around me is crackling, like the delta when a storm is coming from a distance. A light breeze ruffles my hair and sends it across my face. He reaches out and brushes it away, then pulls his hand back as if the gesture surprises him as much as it does me.

The breeze blows again. Too late, I realize it has lifted my top up over my shorts, showing the livid scar that runs across my torso. I go to tug it down, but Antoine's hand stops me.

"What's that?" His hand lingers on the bare skin of my waist, the other resting on the wooden post behind me. He's so close I can breathe him in. The sun catches the gold flecks amid the slate, and beneath his cotton shirt his skin seems to glow burnished brown. I'm so unsettled by being this close to him that my usual stock answers temporarily desert me.

"One of my kidneys was removed."

When he touches the scar it's like a shock against my skin. "Why?"

"Because someone needed it." His finger slowly traces the length of the scar. I'm frozen in place, acutely conscious of its slow pathway around my torso.

"Who?"

"My twin sister. Her name was Tessa." The name sticks in my throat, just as it had in Connor's earlier. It's strange to me that it's now, and to Antoine, I'm saying Tessa's name aloud for the first time since we came here. I don't know him at all. Yet for some reason the words come out, from the place inside me I haven't shared with anyone since Tessa died. It's like the words have a will of their own, reaching toward Antoine and finding form without my conscious agreement. It's unsettling but also oddly comforting, like someone offering you a coat before you've realized you're cold.

An emotion I can't identify moves behind Antoine's eyes. It isn't quite sympathy, but when he takes a step back, something in his posture seems slightly less hard than it did before. He glances at my speaker. "You're listening to Ludovico Einaudi?"

I nod, grateful for the change of subject.

"*I Giorni,*" he says slowly.

"Yes. *The Days,*" I translate.

Antoine's mouth twitches. "Indeed."

He goes to untie the rope anchoring his boat then pauses and looks back at me. "I would rethink your decision in regard to selling, if I were you." He is watching me so closely I can almost feel his eyes on my own.

"Yes." I keep my own tone cool. "You've made your opinion very clear."

He stares at me again, as if I'm a puzzle he's trying to solve. Then he jumps down into the boat, so smoothly it barely causes a ripple on the water and turns the engine on.

He glances up at the jetty. "Goodnight, Harper," he says, oddly formal.

"Goodnight, Antoine."

The boat moves off down the river and I watch it go, frowning.

CHAPTER 5

NIGHTMARES

J don't sleep well that night, or the next one, or the night
after that. It isn't only the encounter with Antoine that
disturbs my peace, though the recollection of his eyes boring into my
own is so disturbing that I turn to digging up the loamy riverside soil
in preparation for a garden rather than think about it. But even
though I go to bed exhausted, the comforting smell of earth under my
nails, it is only to find another, even more disturbing, face when I
sleep.

After appearing under my charcoal without warning, the face from
my sketch seems to have taken up permanent residency in my brain.
In my dreams I'm on the landing at the top of our staircase, staring
into a full-length mirror, and the woman's face is staring back at me.
There is a fire somewhere outside, for flames flicker on the walls, and
the sounds of people screaming echo distantly. The woman's smile is a
cold, cruel grimace. As I stare into the mirror, she begins to laugh. I
jolt awake each day with the maniacal sound still ringing in my ears,
imagining the stench of old fire in my nose.

The dreams aren't the only strange thing. Everything that could go
wrong with our house does that week.

First it's the water. Connor told me it wouldn't be straightforward to get it working, but since then, it's been cracked water main after broken pipe. The city water department isn't cooperating, and every time Connor thinks he's got it fixed, something goes wrong. Then it's the power. We're currently using a generator, but it was supposed to be a temporary measure, and we're both tired of having limited access to electricity. In addition to the restoration, Connor is doing work on other local places and is currently working on a house only one mile from us. "I got the power on there after two days," he says to me one night, his face drawn with frustration when the generator breaks down yet again. "Yet we've been here a month, and I still can't even get a technician to turn it on at the road."

But most annoying of all is the hurricane cellar at the side of the house. "The doors aren't just locked," says Connor one afternoon, showing me where grass and weeds have grown up over the raised concrete block. "They've been cemented shut. Someone really didn't want anyone breaking in."

"Maybe there's treasure down there," I joke.

"Maybe." Connor kicks at the cement in annoyance. "But it's going to be a long, hot job with a jackhammer to get it open. Hurricane season is closing in fast, and we need to have access." He glances at me. "Unless you want to sell. We still haven't talked about it, Harper."

And I still haven't told him about the visit I got from Antoine. I haven't seen or heard from him again, and since my first day, Jeremiah hasn't been in class at all. It's weird. But I don't say any of that to Connor. Instead, I say: "What do you think?"

He sits down on the ground and I sit beside him, playing with a piece of grass. "What I think is that I want us to be happy here," he says quietly. He throws a stone down the hill. "And so far, there's been nothing but drama. First that stupid curse, all the whispers in town. Then these lawyers' letters and that big money offer. Now all the problems just getting the water and power put on." He glances at me. "Maybe I should talk to the grant board and find out if I can redraw the proposal for another one of the old places along the river here. Then we could just sell and buy something else. Something without a curse or a long-lost family member determined to buy it back."

I look down the slope to the water. "If the decision were yours alone," I say slowly, "if I weren't here to influence it—what would you do?"

"That's not fair, Harper. It isn't just my decision."

"But what if it were?" I persist. "Would you stick it out, or would you buy something new?"

He puts a hand out and pulls me to my feet. "I want to show you something." We go in the back of the house, into what used to be the library. Connor walks over to the far wall and presses on the bookcase. Something clicks, and to my amazement, the whole wall swings open, revealing a set of stairs leading down into the darkness. "I followed it most of the way," Connor says, grinning at my face. "It leads to the hurricane cellar, I think, but the door at the bottom is made of reinforced steel. It's also locked. More secrets."

"That's incredible."

"Isn't it?" He swings the shelf back into place and turns to face me. "I know the last thing we need is curses or drama. And that buying a place like this is like strapping a noose around our necks. But if I can pull this off, Harper, there's an entire antebellum trail along here that has funding available for restoration. I'll be earning enough that neither of us ever has to worry again about whether we can afford health insurance. Or college fees."

"Is that all it is, Connor? Is it really just about the money?" I look around at the silent walls. "You could have chosen any of the mansions along here for your plans. But you chose this one. Why?"

Connor nods slowly. "You might not remember this," he says. "But when Tessa was sick, I brought in a stack of photos of the eligible ruins along this part of the river. You picked this one, right away. You said you thought it had something special."

He smiles at my surprise. "I knew you wouldn't remember. But it wasn't just that you liked it. I felt it, too. From the first day I saw it, this house just felt to me like the kind of place families live. After the last two years, neither of us really has a family anymore. Well"—he shrugs—"there's my father, I suppose, but you know Gareth." I do, unfortunately, and I doubt he's had his head out of a bottle long enough to even realize Connor's left Baton Rouge. "This place felt like somewhere to put down roots and stay. I know there's only the two of us left, Harper." He gives me a small smile. "But I guess I want that for us. A home where we can be family to each other. Where we can build families of our own. A place we can always come back to. One where you can paint murals on the walls, and build a greenhouse, maybe even start your own garden center, like you've talked about. And then one day, when your paintings are hanging in a gallery, and you've got a type of rose named after you, you can tell your children about how Uncle Connor and Mom used to camp in the house, when it had nothing more than rotten floorboards and bad skeeters."

It's so unusual for Connor to say anything even remotely sentimental that tears sting my eyes. The picture he paints is one I've barely dared, ever, to allow myself to consider. Somewhere amid losing Mom, then Tessa, the concept of having a family of my own began to seem like a dangerous dream, just one more thing that could be taken away from me. The fact that Connor assumes it is me who would have children and not him is a reminder that I'm not the only one who thinks that way. Connor probably has even more reason than I do to be afraid to dream of a family-filled future, and it's this thought, perhaps more than any other, that dries my tears and stiffens my resolve.

"Then we're not going to sell." I walk through to the kitchen and pick up the papers. "We're going to build a life here, in the mansion we both chose. I'll send these papers back to the lawyers. And we'll just have to brave the curse together."

"Are you really sure?" Connor looks at me worriedly. "Because if we do this, it's not going to be easy, Harper. I have a feeling that cracked pipes and reluctant tradesmen are just the beginning of our problems."

For a moment I see Antoine Marigny's dark eyes. "I'm pretty sure you're right about that." I smile at him. "But let's face it. After the last couple of years, how bad can it really be?"

He smiles wryly. "True." He touches my shoulder. "Sometimes," he says quietly, "I forget you're my younger sister. It's not just what you've been through. You've always been wise. You and Tessa—there are times I think you both came from another place." His hand tightens on my shoulder. "Thank you, Harper."

Unable to speak over the lump in my throat, I cover his hand with my own, and try to push Antoine's face from my mind.

He'll just have to get over it, I think.

CHAPTER 6

WARNING

*I*t takes a couple of days until I get around to going to the lawyers. I'd planned to send the papers by mail, but by now it's the end of the week, and I decide I don't really want to leave it over the weekend. I drive into town early and slip the envelope under the door. I've added a handwritten note to it saying that my brother and I aren't interested in selling—and not to bother sending through any more offers. Something tells me that won't be enough to deter Antoine Marigny, but I figure I should at least try. I'm secretly relieved, though, that I won't be home tonight. I'll be at Avery's house with her and Cass, getting ready for the party out at Perdu Inlet. I suspect that another unscheduled visit might be in the cards after Antoine learns the offer has been rejected.

If I'm honest, I'm more excited about having a real shower than I am about the party. Connor rigged up a makeshift shower in my bathroom from a big drum of water we hauled upstairs, but it falls woefully short of the real thing. Exposed wires hang from the wall where the light should be. I eye them warily when I wash, even though I know they aren't live. A curse is a curse, after all. I've started fantasizing about long, hot showers, so I'll happily pretend to be excited about a party if it means clean hair and shaved legs at last.

At midmorning break I'm heading back out to my car to get a book I forgot, when I see Jeremiah and Antoine standing by the teal Chevy. Even from a distance, I can tell they're arguing. I move a bit closer and stand behind a nearby truck, listening.

"What were your parents thinking?" I hear Antoine say, his voice low and furious. "They knew what would happen if they sold it. This should never have happened." He grips the car door so hard I could swear he's actually bending it.

"The lawyers don't think she'll change her mind. But I'll find a way, Antoine, I promise." Jeremiah's voice sounds scared. "I'll make this right."

"You'll do no such thing." Antoine's voice is grim. "If Harper and her brother haven't changed their minds after the week they've had, they aren't likely to. I'll work it out. Just stay out of my way, and don't do anything stupid." He shakes his head, and Jeremiah walks away, casting nervous looks over his shoulder as he goes. I'm about to follow when Antoine turns around and looks right at me.

"Harper," he says, in a resigned tone, and I wonder how he knew I was there. I step out and face him across a few empty car spaces.

"What did you mean, 'after the week they've had'?" I glare at him. "All the problems with the power company and the water department —they were your doing, weren't they? And Jeremiah—he's just lost both his parents, and here you are, bullying him as well. It's not his fault his parents sold the house."

"His parents knew the house wasn't to be sold." His eyes glint darkly in the sunlight. "They made a mistake that I'm just trying to put right. Jeremiah knows that."

If he's so sure the house shouldn't be sold and has enough money to make the kind of offer he has to Connor and I, why didn't he just buy the house himself? The question hovers in my throat, but asking it feels intrusive and somehow rude, which is odd, given how abrupt his own manner is. Nonetheless, I don't ask it. Outright confrontation has never really been my style.

Stubbornness, though—that, I have down to a fine art. "Well, if you're hoping I'll sell it back to you, I won't."

He's at my side so fast I barely see him move, standing so close it makes me shiver, staring down at me. "You have no idea," he says softly, "what you are playing with. If it's money, then name your price. I don't care how much it is. But believe me, Harper. You do not want to stay in that house. And if you think shower problems are the worst thing you're going to encounter in there, think again."

"Is that a threat?" I don't back away from him. "Because if anything happens to my brother or me, this isn't a very smart conversation for you to be having." He makes an impatient sound and for a moment I think he's going to say something else, then he starts to walk away.

"What's in the hurricane cellar?" I'm not sure what impulse makes me say it, but he stops still, and I can tell by the slow way he turns around that I've hit a nerve. Then he is right in front of me again, unnervingly fast, his face so closed and forbidding I take an instinctive step backward, suddenly very aware that I'm alone in the lot. I'm waiting for some threatening command not to go anywhere near the cellar, but when he does finally speak, his words are completely unexpected.

"How have your dreams been?" His tone is soft, but his eyes boring into mine are dark and turbulent. "That face you sketched. Has it started laughing at you yet?" I'm so taken aback I can't find the words to reply and just stare at him instead. He nods slowly, not taking his eyes away from mine. "I thought so," he says grimly. His mouth is a hard line. "Tell your brother you want to sell, Harper. Sign the house back to Jeremiah and find a new project for your brother to work on. I'll even help you find one. But don't stay in that house."

He starts walking away from me. I'm so shaken from what he's just said that I'm still standing frozen in place, trying to make sense of how he knows about the dreams, when he stops by his Chevy and faces me again. "Jeremiah said there's a party out by the old place on Perdu Inlet tonight. Are you planning on going?"

"Why on earth would it be any of your business if I was?"

His mouth twists in one corner, almost a half smile. "Riverside parties around here have a tendency to get a little rough." His eyes on my face are oddly opaque. "Since you seem to lack a sense of your own mortality, can I offer a second piece of advice and suggest you choose a different way to pass your evening?"

My eyes narrow, and he sighs and shakes his head.

"Well." He pulls the Chevy door open so hard the entire truck shakes. "If you die, I guess at least it will make it easier to buy the damned house back."

CHAPTER 7

PARTY

I'm so excited to have a real shower that for almost a full ten minutes I barely even think about Antoine Marigny. "That," I announce as I come back into Avery's room wrapped in a towel, "was quite seriously the best thing that has happened to me all week."

"No." Avery is pulling all my clothes out of my bag. "The best thing to happen to you will be going shopping for a new wardrobe, but we don't have time to do that right now. There is literally nothing in here suitable for a party." She holds up my jeans and wrinkles her nose in distaste.

I shrug apologetically. "I don't really do dresses."

It's not true. In fact, I used to love dresses, but that was because Tessa usually made them for me. I haven't worn one since she died. Just another thing that leads back to Tessa.

"Tonight, you do. Cass!" With the imperious tone of a sergeant major organizing his troops, she says, "Give Harper the rust-colored one with thin straps. No, that's red, not rust. Yes, that one." She holds it up against me with a critical look. "And a shawl, I think."

"Really?" It's my turn to wrinkle my nose. "Isn't that a bit much for a riverside kegger?"

Cass wags her finger at me. "Always dress for your best night, Harper. Avery's number one rule." She winks at me. "Anyhow, you never know. Jeremiah's sexy uncle might be there." She raises her eyebrows suggestively and I give her a weak smile, as if the sexy uncle hasn't been the only thing I could think about all day.

In the end I give in to their combined ministrations and find myself with my hair up, makeup on, and in strappy heels that I'm sure are going to be tough to navigate outside in the dark. I feel more like I should be going to a cocktail party than the river, but I suspect they've gone overboard in an effort to make me feel welcome, and if I'm honest, there's something genuinely touching about their kindness. Deepwater is a small town, and I'm pretty sure they know at least some of my background by now, but neither of them have asked me any awkward questions and I'm grateful. Cass is driving, so we all pile into her hatchback and head out along the highway to a small back lane, and then onto a pitted dirt road better suited to a truck than a hatch. We make it eventually, coming to a clearing by the river, with a crumbling old house to one side. Despite the warm night, someone has made a bonfire, and I can see kegs stacked up against the ruins. There are more people than I expected, and the moment we step out of the car a plastic cup of beer is in my hand, and some boy I barely recognize in a varsity jacket starts talking to me at high volume about a funny thing he did over the summer.

I nod along and smile in the right places, but I'm not really into it. I'm searching the crowd, but I can't imagine Antoine Marigny at a high school kegger, and I wonder why I should want him to be. I know he's sabotaging our house plans. And somehow, I doubt he's going to just give up.

Cass comes over. "You looked in need of rescuing," she says, drawing me away and looking at me critically as she hands me a fresh cup. "You're not enjoying this." The fragile dress and too much leg are most of the reason I feel uncomfortable, but I don't want to appear ungrateful after their combined efforts.

"I guess I'm worried about our house," I say instead. I remember something Avery said. "Your mom owns a New Age store, right?" Cass nods, looking a little embarrassed. "I know this sounds weird. But do you think she'd answer some questions for me?"

"You mean about the—" Cass turns around to make sure no one is listening and lowers her voice—"curse, right?" I nod and Cass rolls her eyes. "Answer some questions? She'll talk until you can't hear anymore. She'll probably never let you out of the store. Witch Way is open all weekend if you want to go in. I'll let Mom know to expect you, if you'd like."

"That would be great, thanks." I spot Jeremiah over at the other side of the party, looking alone and miserable. He looks up, sees me, and his eyes slide away, clearly uncomfortable. "Excuse me," I say to Cass and make my way around the fire to where he's standing. I've nearly reached him when a burly guy who seems a bit older than the rest of the party steps in my way. "Hey," he says, looking me up and down in a way that makes me wish I'd worn my usual jeans. "I don't know you."

"No." I pull the shawl closer over my chest and try to make my way around him, but he blocks me. "I'm new in town."

"Lucky town," he says, and I don't like the way he's smiling.

"Excuse me." I want to look around to see where Cass and Avery are, but I also don't want to appear scared, so I just keep my eyes down and try again to go around him.

"I know who she is." Another guy is leaning on the first one and gestures to me with his beer cup. "She and her brother bought the old Marigny place." The two of them laugh at that. It isn't a pleasant sound, and I'm starting to get uncomfortable.

"Harper." The two men turn around. Jeremiah is standing behind them. "Are you okay?" His face is as pale and gaunt as ever, and he looks particularly skinny beside the two brawny guys, but there's a certain set to his mouth when he looks at them that makes me think he's not the type to back down.

"Hey, Jeremiah." I skirt neatly around the two guys and link my arm in his. "Good to see you."

"We were talking to her." The original speaker puts a meaty hand on Jeremiah's shoulder, and I see a couple of other men, clearly from the same group, begin to peel away and head toward us.

"Come on, Jeremiah." I tug him away and shoot him a sideways glance that says *pretend they're not there.* We walk away and when they don't follow us, I let out a breath I didn't realize I was holding and smile at Jeremiah. "Thanks," I say, a bit shakily. "I always imagined I'd know how to handle myself in a situation like that."

"You shouldn't have to," he says quietly. "Those guys are jerks."

"Who are they, anyway? They seem a little old for a high school party."

"They're from the bayou over the Louisiana side of the river." Jeremiah gestures at the bridge that crosses the state line. "They're kind of rough, but Jared always invites them because they bring beer and weed." He gestures to the guy in the varsity jacket who'd spoken to me when I first arrived. "Jared Baudelaire. His dad owns half the town."

"Of course he does." I roll my eyes. Jeremiah smiles, and I realize it's the first time I've seen him look even close to relaxed. "I'm glad you're here. I've been trying to find an opportunity to tell you I'm genuinely sorry about the house and everything." His smile is gone as fast as it appeared. "We don't have to talk about it," I add hastily. But it's too late. He's already putting his cup down like he's going to leave.

"This was a mistake," he mutters, turning away. "I shouldn't have come tonight." His eyes meet mine then slide away again. "You shouldn't have, either."

"Why not?" He walks away from the fire and I follow him. "Jeremiah, please. Won't you just tell me what all this is about?" I have to almost run to catch up to him. He's already in the trees and I follow him, leaving the party behind.

"You should get your friends and leave," he says. I can see his motorcycle parked on the other side of the trees by the road. "Those guys from the bayou party pretty hard. Things will likely get wild."

Everything in his manner tells me it's my questions rather than the party Jeremiah is anxious to escape. And also that there is more scaring him than some tough guys from over the state line.

"Jeremiah!" We get to his bike and I tug his arm, so he has to face me. "I overheard you and Antoine in the parking lot this morning. I can tell you're scared of him. Is he threatening you?"

"No. You've got it all wrong, Harper." He's got that tortured look again, as if he's being torn up inside, and he twists his helmet in hands, as if debating what he should say.

"Please. I won't tell anyone. I promise." He opens his mouth. I actually think I might be about to get some answers when suddenly a fist knocks him sideways. I find myself face-to-face with the burly guy from the bayou and belatedly realize three others are standing behind me.

"Don't get up." The man doesn't even look at Jeremiah and instead leers unpleasantly at me.

"Leave her alone." Jeremiah wipes his mouth. I'm looking around for an escape route, but the men are standing between me and the path back to the inlet. Jeremiah struggles to his feet, trying to put himself in between me and the attackers.

"I told you to stay down." The guy nods to his friends and they start laying into Jeremiah with a casual brutality that suggests it's a common pastime.

"Get away from me." I back away and run right into another man, who pushes me toward the first guy, laughing. Jeremiah is curled up in a ball, still taking a beating. I should scream now. I want to. But I can't find my voice and instead I throw my plastic cup of beer at the guy, then make a run for the trees and the party I can still see flickering on the other side of them. I don't make it more than half a step when hands grip me.

"I don't think so," he growls in my ear, holding me from behind. "Where I'm from, girls don't show up to a party in a dress like that unless they want something." I feel a cold trickle of fear down my spine and start to writhe in earnest.

Suddenly the man is wrenched away from me, and a hard arm thrusts me to one side. There is a whirl of movement and a series of grunts, and now it's the two men who were holding me who are on the ground. Antoine Marigny is standing over them with his back to me, fists bunched at his side, and they're staring up at him with terrified expressions. The men who are beating Jeremiah turn around in surprise. One of them runs at Antoine, while another grabs a bottle and raises it. The first guy tackles Antoine, and although he's big and solid, Antoine does something that sends him flying. The second guy brings the bottle crashing down across Antoine's skull, but even as it explodes in a sickening spray of glass and blood, the guy is thrown backward with enough force to make a solid thud as he collides with a tree. Somehow, Antoine is still standing. "Jeremiah," he says without turning around, his voice low and dangerous, "my truck is by the road. Take her home."

Jeremiah takes my arm and pulls me away from the men and the party behind us, through the woods to the road. I think of Cass and Avery, but when I start to mention them, Jeremiah cuts me off abruptly. "You can text them from the car."

I stumble on the uneven ground and when I look behind us, I can see only indistinct shapes in the darkness and hear muffled sounds of pain. Jeremiah opens the truck door and all but pushes me inside. He runs around and jumps in the other side and then we're driving away, and I can't see anything but the road ahead.

CHAPTER 8

QUESTIONS

"We can't just leave him there!" I'm twisting in the seat, trying to look back, but we've already reached the highway. "Jeremiah, he's hurt. Those guys will kill him."

Jeremiah's mouth twists. "I doubt that," he mutters. He looks at me then away again. "Don't worry about Antoine, Harper. He can handle himself."

"You can't be serious." I look at him in astonishment. "There are five of them, and Antoine just had a bottle smashed over his head. How on earth is he going to be fine?" I pull out my phone. "I'm calling 911."

"No." Jeremiah actually grabs the phone out of my hand. "Don't do that, Harper, please. I promise you that Antoine will be fine." He glances at my feet. "You've lost a shoe," he says. "Are you okay?"

"Men are trying to kill your uncle, and you're worried about my lost shoe?" I stare at him, completely baffled.

"Please just trust me." He doesn't meet my eyes. "Antoine will be here soon enough." He's barely finished speaking when a headlight beams through the back, and Jeremiah slows down. "He's got my motorcycle," he says in a relieved tone. He pulls over on the shoulder and opens the cab door, then looks at me. "I know you don't like him," he says quietly. "But you should listen to Antoine. He's just trying to keep you safe, is all."

He gives me a small smile. I hear a murmured exchange, then Antoine folds his length into the driver's seat beside me. Shattered glass glitters in his hair, and there's dirt on his jeans, but apart from that he looks like he just stepped away from having cocktails on the water rather than a fight with five drunken men. He's wearing a loose cotton shirt over faded jeans, and I can't see any mark at all where the bottle caught his head. He pulls the door closed and rests one hand loosely on the steering wheel as he waits for Jeremiah to mount his bike. He glances down at my feet and frowns. "You shouldn't be bare-foot in here," he says. "There's broken glass."

I stare at him with the same disbelief I did Jeremiah. "Broken glass from a bottle that smashed on your head. You shouldn't even be standing."

He shrugs, looking in the rearview mirror. He waits for Jeremiah to ride past us before he pulls out onto the road. "The bottle broke before it hit my head. I just got some glass spray."

"Glass spray?" I shake my head. "I saw it, Antoine. That bottle hit you so hard it shattered."

"I'm fine." He nods at my phone. "You should text your friends. I told them that Jeremiah took you home, but they're probably a little uneasy."

I pull out my phone and send a message to Cass and Avery saying that Jeremiah needed to talk and has taken me home, but I barely notice what I'm typing. Headlights come toward us and in their glare, I see a stain on the far collar of Antoine's shirt. I frown. "Is that blood?" I lean closer and he pulls away, giving me a look that sends me back to my side of the bench seat.

"I'm fine." He changes gears like he wants to hurt the truck. "I did mention that party would be a bad idea," he says in a milder tone.

"Is that really all you're going to say?" I turn on the bench seat and stare at him. "Nothing about how you just fought off five angry, drunk men and the blood stain on your collar?"

"The blood isn't mine."

"Really," I say sarcastically. "That's the best you can do?"

He raises his hand from the steering wheel in a dismissive gesture I find infuriating and half smiles at me.

The reality is I don't know what to think. I guess it's possible I could be mistaken in what I saw. Somehow, though, I don't think so. I think there is a whole story I'm not seeing, and it makes me uneasy.

"How is it that you just happened to be at the party?" I glare at him. "Are you stalking me?"

"Coincidence. I like to keep an eye out for Jeremiah." He shoots me a sideways glance, that same maddening smile still on his face.

I fold my arms and stare out the window. "It's time you gave me some real answers."

"There's only one answer that matters." He takes the turn onto the road that leads to my house. "The word *yes* and your signature on the title deed for my family's house."

When I roll my eyes, he smiles, and I'm annoyed as hell because despite everything, I find myself wanting to smile back. Antoine might make me uneasy, but he fascinates me in equal measure. "Look. It isn't just my decision. My brother worked for months on the proposal for that house. It's a dream come true for him. He loves it."

"And you love your brother."

I nod. "I do."

"I respect that." He takes a beat, as if he's considering his next words carefully. "I'm not trying to ruin your brother's dream, Harper, or yours. I understand this must seem confusing, and that you want answers. But there are some things I can't explain, and I need you to hear me when I say that it is better for both of you if I don't. I wish you would also believe me when I say that neither of you is safe so long as that house is in your name."

"Are you trying to blame what happened tonight on me owning your family home?"

"No." He shakes his head. "Tonight, at least, was entirely unrelated."

At least, I think. Which means that other things are related. But what things? And how?

"If it was entirely unrelated, why did you tell me earlier not to go?"

LUCY HOLDEN

I have my back against the door, watching him, and it would be easier to maintain my hard line of questioning if he didn't look so amused by the things I say. The way his mouth half smiles at every one of my questions sends an unwelcome thrill down my spine.

"Those parties are never a good idea." His eyes flicker sideways. "Particularly when you look that beautiful in a dress."

"You didn't know I'd wear a dress," I say lamely.

He laughs low in his throat, and I feel my stomach flip over. "Let's just say it wasn't hard to imagine."

"So, you're saying I can't go to a party in a dress and be safe? Don't you think that's a little old-fashioned?"

This time his laugh is genuine. "Maybe it is." He tilts his head as if at a private joke. "But I do think that such a beautiful dress deserves a better night out than a bayou kegger."

Since I had thought exactly the same thing, it's hard to argue. I change the subject. "Are you going to tell me what happened with those guys back there?" I know he won't, but I can't let it go.

"I made a convincing argument that the other side of the state border might be a better place to spend the remainder of their evening." He turns into the oak-covered driveway.

"And they just agreed to leave." Something about the lighthearted way he deflects the question makes me even more certain there is a great deal he isn't saying.

He lifts one shoulder. "After a little discussion."

I try not to imagine what form that discussion took. Instinct tells me very little of it was verbal. Which brings me back to how Antoine took on an entire group of men without sustaining any real injury, which in turn brings back that uneasy feeling.

Connor's truck is parked outside, and he's sitting on the porch by the hurricane lamp squinting at the headlights. He would never tell me not to go to a party, but I suspect he never goes to sleep until he knows I'm home. It should be annoying, but if I'm honest, it's kind of touching. Antoine parks the truck and turns the engine off.

"You should probably go," I say hastily. Connor and I haven't had any real reason so far to have the dating discussion, but something

44

tells me that Antoine Marigny might not be the best place to begin when we do. His door is already open, though, and with that unnerving swiftness, Antoine is around and opening mine before I've finished speaking. I glare at him as I step out then wince when my bare foot lands on a sharp stone. "Ow." I lean down to examine my foot, grimacing as blood starts to drip from it. "Connor," I call out. "Can you get my boots? I've cut my foot." I look up and there must be a trick of the light, because for a moment it seems as if Antoine's eyes are actually gleaming in the dark, like some kind of lethal animal.

Then he turns away and when I look up again, Connor is walking toward me carrying my old Ariats, and Antoine is gone, around the other side of the truck, his face hidden from view.

"Harper." Connor hands me the boots, frowning at Antoine's figure. "What happened?"

"Nothing. My shoe broke, and Antoine gave me a ride home. I just landed on a stone, is all." I wince as I pull on the boots and stand up.

"Antoine?" Connor's eyes move between us. "As in Marigny?"

Antoine holds out his hand, but I notice he is keeping a distance from me, and he stays in the shadow of the truck. "You must be Connor," he says.

"And you must be the guy who's been making my life difficult." Connor takes the hand but there's nothing friendly in his voice. Antoine steps into the light and his face is perfectly normal. He's even smiling. He looks like he always does, ready to hang glide off the nearest cliff or rappel down it, but not remotely more threatening than that. He looks like someone Connor would be friends with, not like a predator about to strike.

"Now that my sister has made it perfectly clear that we don't want to sell," Connor says coldly, "maybe you'll stop interfering with the water department and whoever else you've been bribing around town."

Antoine seems more amused than annoyed. "No," he says mildly. "I won't stop. But I can offer you more money to sell if you like. Whatever it takes." He nods at the hurricane lamp. "I'd make a decision soon though. It's not safe living in a house with no water and kerosene lanterns."

Connor stares at him. "You're admitting to bribery and harassment —and telling me that I can expect it to continue?"

Antoine leans against his truck with folded arms. "That's about it. Unless you agree to sell, of course. Then you'll discover how effective I can be as a friend. There are dozens of antebellum ruins along this part of the river. I'll make sure you have the pick of them. And enough money to turn it into a showpiece. Ensure your power and water go on easily."

Connor folds his own arms and looks back at him stubbornly. "We're never going to sell."

"Never is a very long time, friend." Antoine peels his long body off the truck and moves around to the driver's door. "Oh," he says as he reaches it, his eyes resting briefly on me. "And if I were you, I'd take better care of your sister. Kegger parties out at Perdu tend to attract a bit of a rough crowd." His mouth curves at my indignation, as if he knows exactly how annoyed I am. "But you do look beautiful in that dress," he says as he starts the engine. Now his smile is unmistakable.

He nods at Connor from behind the wheel, and then he's gone.

Connor waits until the lights disappear down the drive then turns a furious face to me. "Do I even want to know how he came to be the one who drove you home?"

"Nope." I start limping toward the house. "Nor do you want to give me lectures about kegger parties by the river or wearing dresses to them. Because we're both going to agree that tonight was a bust, and then we're going to go to bed, and we're not going to think about the fact that Antoine Marigny seems determined to either get his house back or destroy us in the process."

CHAPTER 9

CELLAR

*C*onnor takes the hint. He and I go to bed that night without talking about Antoine or what we're going to do, but we both know we're going to need to talk about it eventually. I close my eyes. I can't even begin to think about what happened at the party. It seems to have taken place behind a curtain I'm not ready to peer behind. I became accustomed long ago to compartmentalizing things I'd rather not dwell on.

I can feel the customary nightmares hovering, but they seem a less dangerous alternative than my conscious mind. Besides, I'm so tired and confused I can barely hold my lids open. I sink into sleep despite myself, hoping that just this once the dreams might leave me alone.

I must sleep for a time, because when the first hint of the woman enters my dreams, I don't immediately recognize what's happening. But then come the familiar scenes of flames beyond the window and people screaming out, and finally, her face appears, floating into the dream exactly as I drew it, but alive somehow, as if she is both drawing and person. She looks as if she's in pain, and she's reaching for me, trying to say something. "What is it?" I ask in my dream. "What do you want?"

"Help." The word is a hoarse whisper, as if it takes all of her energy to say it. "Help us." Her face disappears, replaced by a flash of darkened stairs and a thick door. Then it reappears, clearer this time, and when she speaks her voice sounds stronger. "Help us, please."

I jerk awake. The river breeze stirs the mosquito nets around my bed, and through the open windows a high moon is shining. I get out of bed and walk over to the window, taking deep breaths of the warm night air, trying to steady my heart. Petals drift from the red magnolia by the dock, gleaming crimson under the moon as they fall on the water like drops of blood. For a moment it seems like something moves beneath the branches, but I look at the same place until my eyes strain, and I don't see it again.

I sit on the window seat, thinking of the dream, the woman's voice, and the stairs. *I know those stairs.* They're the ones behind the shelf in the library that Connor showed me.

I know I won't be able to sleep again, so I pad downstairs and go through the house to the library. Moonlight streams through the open windows, and again I think I see something move beyond them, feel a rush of air nearby, but when I swing around there's nothing, and I chide myself for jumping at shadows.

It takes me a while to find the button Connor pressed and when I do, the bookshelf makes such a loud creaking noise that I wince, worried Connor will wake. I wait a moment, but I don't hear anything. I pause at the stairs and shine my phone light down them. The air coming up seems very cold, which makes sense, I guess, since it would be cooler underground. I hesitate for a moment. Going down a secret staircase to a locked cellar in the middle of the night because a woman whispered to me in a dream definitely doesn't sound like the most rational decision. But then I think of Antoine asking me how my dreams have been, and my lips tighten.

Nobody wants something as badly as he wants this house unless they've got something to hide. Maybe I've known it all along, and that's why I haven't wanted to just give in, even though I know that taking the money is the smart thing to do. He's hiding something. And whatever it is has something to do with the cellar at the bottom of these stairs.

RED MAGNOLIA

I prop the bookshelf open with an old chair, take a deep breath, and start going down the stairs.

There's a strange smell on the air and my nose wrinkles. It smells like the fire in my dream, long gone cold. Charred and acrid. The further I go on, the more the scent grows. I don't remember smelling it when Connor opened the bookshelf before, but perhaps it's the night moisture that brings it out.

The staircase reaches a landing. I look back up, but the bookshelf is wide open, and I can still see the moonlight spilling across the floor. The staircase switches and goes down another level. I shine my phone down it and see the door Connor mentioned. It's a huge steel thing, like he described, with thick reinforcement across it that looks like iron. A strange symbol is embossed in the center, a square with loops at each corner and what looks like a sun in the middle. Iron bars stretch from it to each side, sealing the door utterly closed.

"You really don't want anyone going into that cellar, do you, Antoine," I murmur. The air is colder down here, and the charred smell is getting thick enough to taste. I reach out hesitantly and put my hand on the door. It's so cold it almost hurts, and I pull my hand back, startled, then tentatively touch it again. It isn't my imagination. The door feels like the inside of a freezer. I half expect my hand to stick to it like ice. I move closer, and put my ear to the door, then realize how ridiculous it is to be trying to listen to a cellar that's clearly been shut for years, if not decades.

Except then I hear the whisper, just like in my dream. "Help." It's not really a whisper anymore. It's a real voice, a woman's voice. I stare at the door in horror.

"Hello?" My voice sounds awfully loud in the dark space. "Are you there?"

"Help us," comes the voice again, but it's faded, like it's taken all her strength to speak.

"I will!" I shine the light all over the door trying to find where I unlock it. "Can you tell me how to get you out? Tell me what to do to help you."

"Cold," says the voice, and now it is fading into a thin whisper. "So cold." It is cold, I realize, and not just the door.

"Wait! I'm going to get my brother, and we're going to get you out of there. Just hold on." I turn back and begin to run up the stairs, heart pounding furiously, not daring to even think about what kind of man kept an actual person locked in the cellar—nor how we could have been in the house so long without even knowing she was there.

That thought makes me stop. *It isn't possible. Nobody could have survived under there for over a month without us knowing.*

I'm scared. Every instinct is telling me to run. But something deeper knows that if I do, I will lie awake for the rest of the night, terrified and wondering. Another part of me knows that so much as mentioning this to Connor will mean those papers are signed as soon as the attorneys open on Monday. That is, if he doesn't have me committed for insanity.

Maybe I could wait for daylight. Everything is less frightening during the day. But then I wonder if maybe the voice will be gone by then and all this nothing more than a dream I imagined. Eventually I come back to my earlier conclusion that leaving now will just drive me crazy. I turn around reluctantly, still unconvinced I'm doing the right thing, and walk slowly back down to stand in front of the door.

I lift my phone up and press the voice recorder. "Are you really there?" The jagged audio line spikes at the sound of my voice.

"Help us," comes the soft whisper, just as it has before. I look at the line on my phone.

It isn't moving.

"Who are you?" I'm barely able to whisper. The line on the voice app surges in jagged streaks as I speak, responding to even my softest voice.

"Help us." The line on the phone stays completely flat, not even the faintest movement indicating sound.

"You're not real," I whisper. "You're in my head." I turn and stumble over the landing in my haste to get out of there, my earlier fears overwhelming me. I'm terrified, my mind whirling in confusion, and suddenly I can't scramble up the stairs fast enough. I take them in a series of leaps and fall into the library, kicking the chair away and pushing the bookshelf closed, desperate to get away from the dark passage and the smell of old fire.

CHAPTER 10

HISTORY

J don't sleep a wink for the rest of the night. I'm so terrified
of what is below the house that I can't bear to think of it, so
instead I pull back the curtain and hit replay on the scene at the party,
which seems markedly less terrifying after what I've just experienced.
I play it over and over, trying and failing to make sense of what I saw.
That bottle smashed over Antoine's head. The looks of terror on the
men's faces, all five of them, all big men.

None of it makes any sense.

I'm glad Antoine appeared when he did. Even if I don't particularly
relish the role of damsel in distress, I shudder to contemplate what
might have happened if Antoine hadn't intervened. The memory of
being surrounded by drunk men who clearly had more in mind than a
social chat isn't pleasant. I don't let myself dwell on the fear, however.
Partly because I learned a long time ago to be grateful for the bad
things that don't happen, just as much as the good things that do. And
not least because by comparison with what happened after Antoine
arrived, and then later in the cellar, those earlier fears seem almost
mundane. Men with dark agendas are ugly and unpleasant, but they're
also part of the world we all live in. Antoine's ability to fight them all
off single-handedly, disembodied voices whispering in the middle of

the night—those are something else entirely. Something I neither understand nor can even begin to make sense of.

I wash under the makeshift shower early the next morning, and when Connor comes downstairs, I'm sitting on the porch. I don't want to be inside. Whatever is downstairs, I need to find out what it is —and if it is able to hurt my brother or me.

"I have to head into town this morning for lumber and a few other things," Connor says, throwing me an apple and biting into one himself. "You could ride in with me and pick up your car from wherever you left it."

"Thanks." I follow him out. "About last night," I say as we get into the truck. "I'm sorry about how I was when I came home. Some guys from over the state border were at the party. Antoine was dropping his nephew off and saw them bothering me. If I'm honest, I was lucky he was there." At least that part isn't a lie. I *was* lucky he was there. More could have been ruined than my dress if he hadn't.

"He's not exactly who I would have picked as hero material," says Connor dryly.

"No." I think back to the ruthless efficiency with which my attackers had been dispatched, how they had backed away in fear when Antoine faced them. "More mercenary than hero, I suspect."

Connor clears his throat. "He's a little, ah, older than the usual crowd I'd expect to see at a high school kegger."

"I have no idea how old he is." I stare straight ahead.

"Well, if you plan on seeing any more of him, you might want to find that out. I don't want to be your keeper, Harper." Connor looks uncomfortable. "But much as I hate to admit it, Marigny had a point. Maybe next time you plan on going to a party like that we should talk about it. At least work out a deal between us so that if you are in trouble, I can help you."

"That's fair." He nods, and that's the end of it. I like that about Connor and me, the way we can resolve stuff without drama. I wait a little. "Hey, Connor. Have you had any weird dreams since we moved into the house?"

"Dreams?" The corners of his mouth turn down and he shakes his head. "I never really remember my dreams. Why?" He gives me a concerned look. "Are you having trouble sleeping?"

"No," I say quickly, wanting to head that one off at the pass. "Not at all. I just had a couple of restless nights." Thankfully, he lets it go for the rest of the way into town.

We drive into the lumberyard, and I stay in the truck while Connor talks to the foreman. A medium-sized flatbed with Louisiana plates pulls in beside me. When the passengers climb out, I nearly faint from shock.

It's the bayou guys from the night before, and they look like hell.

They wince as they step down. The two guys who had bounced me between them are clutching their ribs, their faces so swollen and stitched they're barely recognizable. "What happened to you?" I hear the foreman ask, looking at them in astonishment.

"Car wreck," mumbles the man who'd first blocked my path, eyes downcast. "Can't hardly remember it."

"Car wreck!" One of the other men in the truck, a face I don't recognize from last night, hoots with laughter. "My sister works nights at the ER. Way I heard it, you boys were found sitting in the middle of the road, naked as the day you were born and lost as last year's Easter egg. Don't even want to know how y'all wound up in a car wreck with no clothes."

"That's just talk," said the first man sullenly. "Or someone's sick idea of a joke. Police told me they got an anonymous 911 call, otherwise we'd have been in real trouble. Don't remember nothin' but waking up in the ER and finding out my truck was wrapped around a tree."

I remember the murmured conversation when Antoine passed Jeremiah on the road and the direction his headlights took when he left our house last night. I have a sneaking suspicion that having them found butt naked in the middle of the road is exactly Antoine's idea of a joke. And I'd put money on it those guys had nothing to do with their truck being wrapped around a tree. *But surely they'd remember Antoine—and me?*

An odd recklessness takes hold of me. I step out of the car and walk over to Connor, straight past the Louisiana men. "Good morning," I say politely as I pass them, making sure they get a good look at my face.

"Morning." They return the greeting without a trace of recognition. Emboldened, I look directly at them. "Wow. You guys sure look like you've had a rough night."

"Yeah." The man who'd originally confronted me looks a little shamefaced. "Last time we drink and drive, boys, isn't that what we agreed?" There's a general murmur of agreement, but again, not a hint of recognition.

"Well," I say over my shoulder as Connor pays for the lumber. "Take care of yourselves." I give them one last look. Nope. Not a thing.

My head is spinning. When Connor drops me at Avery's place, I'm almost relieved that the house is silent, and she still hasn't answered my text. She's clearly sleeping, and I'm not interested at all in talking. I'm glad I had my car keys with me last night. I tell Connor I'll be home later and drive down Main Street, then down West, until I come to a stop outside a stately old home with a sign that says Deepwater Hollow Historical Society.

I want some answers.

The lady behind the desk is very helpful. "I've already given your brother everything I have on the mansion's original floor plan," she says after I introduce myself. "Such a magnificent building. We're all very happy that it's being salvaged. It's stood a ruin for so long now." She shakes her head disapprovingly.

"Actually, it's more the family history I was interested in. I wondered what you might have on the Marignys themselves. Did they always own the house?"

"Oh, now, let's see." The lady looks absolutely thrilled at the challenge. "The Marignys were one of the original families to settle here, you know, back when Mississippi was a French colony. They are mentioned in all the early records, particularly in relation to negotiations with the Natchez people in the area." She puts a hand over her mouth and looks around as if she's going to say something scandalous. "In fact, it's whispered that one of the earliest family members made the negotiations a little personal, if you take my meaning." She winks too obviously for her meaning to possibly be missed. She takes me into a back room. "We keep an archive of all the original documents pertaining to the first families. Most of it has been digitized now, of course, so if you don't mind the mess, you can look through it yourself once I unlock the folder for you."

I thank her and sit down to scroll through it. Many of the documents are titles and deeds, showing the extent of the Marigny holdings, which were grand by any standards. I find the original grant for the land our house stands on and discover it was a cotton plantation. It seems the Marignys had a hand in every battle or business deal that happened around Deepwater. The lady was right—in all the negotiations with the Natchez, the Marigny name pops up. I come to a document dated 1731 and freeze. It's a truce between a local Natchez chief, known as the Great Sun, and Antoine Marigny. But it isn't the name that makes my heart stop. It's the symbol below the signatures: a square with loops at each corner and a sun in the center. Exactly the same as the one on the door at the entrance to the cellar.

The truce is written in old-fashioned French, and my hands are shaking so much it takes me a while to make sense of it, but in the end, I gather that an Antoine Jacques Marigny promised to vanquish a "Great Enemy" of the Natchez. In return, he was inducted into the tribe itself and given a "totem."

I take a photo of the symbol on my phone.

I scan the rest of the documents, but I can't find anything mentioning a curse of any kind, or any other mention of the totem. Antoine could be a family name, I tell myself. The Marigny family seems to have had mixed fortunes, declining, like most in the South, I guess, after the Civil War. The house remained in the family, but the wealth it once held faded with the glory days of cotton and tobacco.

I find only one other document that might help. It is a letter from a French officer to his superior and dated several weeks after the truce, still in 1731. It describes a slave uprising at the Marigny estate. "There was a terrible sickness, and the slaves died in their dozens," it reads.

"When they finally rose against their masters, they took a terrible revenge."

I frown, using an online translator when my own very basic French fails. "Fire consumed the fields," I read, "and men fled in terror from the demons that came to kill them. The land around was charred black, and for months a terrible cold lay upon the air."

I think of the darkened stairs leading to the cellar beneath our house, the charred scent of old fire, and the terrible cold I felt through the door. A tongue of fear licks at my spine.

What if the demons that came to kill the Marignys are the same ones whispering to me in the night? I push the chair back, suddenly anxious to get out of there. What if Antoine Marigny's warnings mean something after all?

I push open the door, close my eyes, and inhale the warm, fragrant summer air with a relief that lasts until I open my eyes, and find Antoine Marigny standing right in front of me.

CHAPTER 11

MYTH

"*D*eveloped a sudden interest in history?" Antoine is holding two coffees. He hands me one, then leans up against the driver's side of my car, doing the arms-folded thing he seems to do whenever we talk.

"We're coffee buddies now?"

He raises his eyebrows at me, with that half smile that's starting to really get under my skin. "Just being neighborly."

I glare at him and reach for the door, but he's leaning in a way that holds it closed. He's wearing a blue cotton shirt that makes his eyes vivid and endless as the Gulf of Mexico, and the way he wears jeans is starting to bother me. "Move," I say curtly.

"Rude." He slides sideways just enough that I have to press up against him to put my key in the door. I try to ignore the way he feels against me, lean and taut, like a mountain lion about to pounce.

"I saw your friends from the party at the lumberyard this morning." I give him a pointed look. "Apparently they were found naked on the road. Their car was wrapped around a tree, and they woke up in the ER after someone called 911."

Antoine takes a leisurely sip of coffee. "Pity," he murmurs.

"Pity that they wrapped their car around a tree, or that someone called 911?"

"Pity that they woke up." I roll my eyes. He sips his coffee and watches me with that same maddening smile.

"I left out the most interesting part." I cross my own arms and stare at him, the open car door between us. "None of them showed even the faintest sign of knowing who I was."

"And you in that beautiful dress." He grimaces. "*Quelle horreur.*"

"That." I seize on it. "That right there." He gives me an innocent look. "You speak French."

"One phrase is not French." But his eyes narrow slightly. He unfolds himself and steps away from the vehicle, and I smile to myself. I'm getting closer to the truth. "I'm going to get answers," I say, sliding into the driver's seat and looking up at him. "Whether you want me to find them or not." For a moment I think of telling him about my sleepless night and the whispers in the cellar, but then I think of the men I saw this morning, the way they didn't recognize me at all, and I think better of it. I will get to the bottom of the mystery that is Antoine Marigny. But I don't intend to give him any chance to mess around with my thoughts. Whatever he did to those men isn't something I want to find happening to me. For all I know, he could convince me to believe that I never owned the mansion at all.

I start to reverse and he holds up a hand. I put my head out of the window and give him my most imperious stare. "What?"

He points to the ground. "Your Mustang has an oil leak. It's a common problem in that model."

"An oil leak. Really?"

"That car is a classic. It pains me to see it hurt." He opens his hands in a helpless gesture.

"You are unbelievable, you know that?" He grins, openly this time, and I turn my head and reverse the car.

"Where to now, Nancy Drew?" he calls as I straighten up.

"None of your business." I accelerate with a little more force than necessary and leave him standing in the road, which would be a whole lot more satisfying if he weren't still grinning at me. I go up Main and turn into Third Street. Cass's mom's store is on the right, a sweet little place with wind chimes out front and a huge crystal ball in the window. The sign in the window says Witch Way. The play on words couldn't be more appropriate, I think grimly, as I open the door. I turn to close it, and Antoine Marigny is waving at me from the other side of the street.

There's no way he got here that fast on foot. He's not even trying to pretend to be normal anymore. That thought should be terrifying, I guess. Instead I'm intrigued and completely unable to stop my search. I have the sense of being on a runaway train, headed toward a destination I both want to find and dread arriving at. It's oddly exhilarating and equally frustrating.

I suppress a childish desire to stick my tongue out at him and settle for glaring instead.

Bells hanging over the door clang together in a not unpleasant sound as I go into Witch Way, smiling at the lady behind the counter, who I assume is Cass's mom.

"Harper." Cass's mom is like imagining Cass twenty years into the future, her smile just as open and welcoming as her daughter's is. "I'm Selena." The pile of braids on her head is even taller than Cass's and wrapped in a bright orange scarf, beneath which she wears dangling silver earrings. She gestures at my car. "Cass told me you drive a pink Mustang convertible," she says, explaining why she knows my name. "She also said you'd be coming by to see me." She looks past me out the window and frowns. "Did Antoine Marigny come here with you?"

"No. Just ignore him." She gives me a curious look. "He wants to buy my house. We don't really see eye to eye on it."

"I see," she says, in a tone that says she really doesn't. Thinking it prudent to change the subject, I say, "Cass tells me you might be able to help with the curse on the Marigny mansion."

"Ah." She looks at me in a way that says she won't say anymore until I do.

"I don't actually know what the curse is," I say. "But since I've been in the house, I've had really bad dreams." She's looking at me closely and I drop my eyes. "It's the same dream," I say. "A woman's face. She's asking me for help."

"Is that all?"

I give a half-hearted shrug and look away. "More or less."

"I see." Selena watches me. "Well, a lot of the old houses here have magic attached to them. Did you know this was once Natchez territory?"

"I've just been learning about it."

"Right. Well, the Natchez were one of the most powerful of the Native American nations, with a fascinating history. Their chiefs were known as the Great Sun. Each was born of the daughter of the last Great Sun, so it was a matrilineal culture."

She pauses. "You need to stop me if I get boring, Harper. Cass will tell you that I can talk about this stuff all day."

"It's fine." I want to tell her that the relief of talking to someone who doesn't think my dreams are crazy or even unusual is like finding cool water in the desert. "Please, talk away. It's my home now, and I'll take any advice you might have to offer."

"Okay. But stop me if it's too much." She leans on the glass countertop. "The Natchez believed that marrying outside of their own tribe strengthened their blood, so they made alliances with outsiders —even with white men. In the early days of Deepwater, there were many marriages between the French settlers and the Natchez. Whenever that happened, so the legends go, the Natchez would weave their own magic into the lands the French took. Then, later, the slaves came, and brought magic of their own. So, this part of Mississippi became a place where all that magic intersected." She shrugs. "Most people think it's just fancy and superstition. But they were savage days. Blood was spilled and stakes were high. Such times make a mark upon the land, as do those whose histories are interwoven with it. The curse on your house goes back to those times."

"But what is it, exactly?"

Her mouth purses and I get the feeling she's weighing her words carefully. "Sometimes magic is given to a certain person, or a certain family, to hold. A long time ago, something terrible happened on Marigny land."

I nod. "A sickness," I say. "I read about it at the historical society. Dozens died, and there was a slave uprising against their masters."

"Not a sickness." Selena's voice is hard. "A massacre. The Marignys were sadists. They were known as heartless masters who abused their slaves terribly. Perhaps it was the isolation, perhaps they were simply mad with power, but by all accounts, they descended into insanity, even forcing some of the slaves to torture and kill their own. At night there were wild, savage parties in the mansion. Chaos. Blood in the fields. The slaves feared they would all fall prey to the madness, or worse, become creatures of it themselves. They rose up against the family, intending to kill them all. But somewhere amid the chaos, the Marigny family, or the so-called demons who worked for them, made the mistake of massacring the inhabitants of a Natchez settlement. That was when the Natchez intervened."

"The truce?"

She nods. "A Natchez woman claimed that the Marignys had been affected by a curse, a form of insanity that would continue to spread and infect others unless it was contained. She said she could make the killings stop, but only by binding the curse to the family itself. A deal was struck with Antoine Marigny, a son of the plantation owner: the family would be allowed to live if he took the curse into his body. The stories say that the son had close ties with the Natchez that made them trust him, though of course those are just stories. Whatever the truth, the stories say that the Natchez planned for the curse to be bound to him, rendering the demons unable to hurt anyone else. The Natchez woman created a powerful totem, a symbol to bind the curse, and the truce was signed. The Marignys were spared."

The symbol I saw earlier on the paper outlining the truce crosses my mind. I take out my phone and show Selena the photo I took of it. "A totem like this?"

"A totem exactly like that." She nods slowly, staring at it. "Where did you get this?"

"The historical society. There's a copy of the truce there."

Selena's face lights up as if I've said the most interesting thing she's heard all year. "I never even thought to check for actual records. I must go and have a look."

I'm less interested in the historical records, however, than whatever the actual curse is on my house.

"But if the killings were stopped, how is it that the house is still cursed?"

"The Natchez woman captured the magic inside the Marigny boy himself, but it wasn't destroyed. The stories say it drove him mad, made him the worst of them all." Selena looks at me. "The demons had to be contained, locked away. That's where my people came in."

"Your people?"

She gives me a wry smile. "My family began their lives here as slaves on the Marigny estate. Our stories say that my ancestor, Samuel, was a medicine man back in the Caribbean. He knew different magic from the Natchez. Darker, in some ways. Blood magic. What people these days might call voodoo—although we've never called it that. It's a force connected to water, shared by all beings."

"So you know what happened? You understand what they did?" I feel a surge of excitement that I might finally have some answers that is dashed when Selena shakes her head.

"Not really. I'm sorry to disappoint you, Harper, but for all my interest in my own history, there's very little I know for fact. And any rituals I might practice now are only experiments, lighthearted fun." She opens her hands in a equivocal gesture. "All I know are stories that have been handed down. They're no more, really, than myth now. The stories say that without certain totems, the demons couldn't survive in sunlight. Everyone knew they preferred the nights. It was rumored they spent most of the daylight hours asleep beneath the mansion itself. My ancestor, the story goes, used his magic to steal the totems just before dawn, when the demons were distracted, reckless after a night of wild debauchery. He waited until they had retreated beneath the house to sleep, and then he and the Natchez woman worked a piece of blood magic, a binding spell that linked the curse not only to the demons' bodies but to the Marigny land and to the house itself, binding it inside that building so long as a living Marigny owns it, and Natchez blood seals it."

I absorb the picture her words paint in my mind, trying to ignore the choking fear unspooling in my belly. When I speak my voice sounds slightly choked: "And when a living Marigny no longer owns it?"

She looks at me soberly. "Then there's nothing left to hold the darkness captive. It's free to escape."

"And kill people," I whisper. "Like Jeremiah's parents."

"Perhaps." Selena leans over the counter and takes my hands. "But Harper," she says gently, "these are old stories. Myths. I know how frightening they sound, but in the end that's all they are—stories." She lets my hands go. "I told you all I know about the curse because I think that if you own the mansion, you have a right to know. But that doesn't mean I believe in it." She smiles gently. "And sometimes, dreams are just dreams. Not everything has a deeper meaning."

I nod slowly. "What happened to the rest of the family?"

"Most had the sense to move away." She shrugs. "Those who stayed kept to themselves. There were always rumors of madness in the Marigny family, whether true or superstition. The family fortunes came and went, as did most in the South. Eventually what wealth was left was gone, and any sign of former glory lost with it. But no matter how poor they were, until Jeremiah's parents, the Marignys never sold the house itself. This is the Deep South, after all." She shrugs. "Old superstitions die hard. An old trust fund paid the land taxes every year, and although there was never enough to restore it, the mansion remained in the Marigny family."

"Until me."

"Yes," says Selena quietly. "Until you."

I give her a small smile. "Thank you," I say, meaning it. "I guess it's good, at least, to know the truth."

I walk toward the door and the light outside, trying to ignore the cold fear churning inside.

CHAPTER 12

SCARS

When I go outside, the Mustang's hood is up, and Antoine has his hands in the engine. I inhale sharply, unwilling to let him see my discomfort.

"What do you think you're doing?" It's my turn to fold my arms.

He twists his head sideways and smiles crookedly. "Like I said, it's a classic. When it hurts, I hurt with it. I could fix that leak for you if you like." He drops the hood.

"Why are we suddenly friends?" I ask. I don't feel like being light-hearted anymore. Not after Selena's story.

Shadows chase the humor from his face. "Because I need you to trust me," he says quietly. "And going by your errands this morning, I think perhaps you are beginning to see why."

"What I'm beginning to see is that you have a lot of secrets. All of this would be much easier if you just told me the truth."

"Ah. The truth." His tone is mocking, his eyes hooded. I sigh and reach over to put my bag in the back.

When I turn back he has moved to stand directly in front of me, one hand resting on the car roof so I'm almost in his embrace. "And what is it that you think the truth is?"

"You ask a lot of questions." He's too close, his eyes dark and unsettling. He smells of cedar and cypress, and I can barely breathe. "And you don't answer any of mine."

"Perhaps that's because I think it's safer for you if I don't."

"I don't need you to keep me safe."

The hand that isn't on the roof touches the scar on my torso, tracing it lightly through my T-shirt. I freeze, barely able to breathe, unbearably aware of his touch through the cotton top. "I would debate that." His hand stills, and he holds my eyes. "Please, Harper, for once just trust me. The safest thing for you to do is to drop this—and sell me the mansion."

I shake my head and turn so he is forced to step away. As he lifts his hand from the Mustang and turns, his shirt lifts slightly, revealing a tattoo right at the base of his spine. I stop with my hand in midair, staring at it in shock. He glances back and frowns when he sees my face.

"What is it?"

"Your tattoo." My voice is unsteady.

"It's nothing. A stupid teenage thing," he says curtly. His face has shut down like a screen that's been switched off.

"It's not nothing." I hold up my phone so he can see the screenshot I took earlier. "It's the totem the Natchez gave to your family."

"You really have been doing your homework," he says flatly.

"What does it mean?"

He turns away briefly, as if to gather himself. When he meets my eyes again, his face is bland. "It means that I used to be an idiot who wanted to impress girls, with a family who, as it turns out, were most definitely not worth the trouble." He smiles with light amusement, any trace of concern gone. "And if you really want to understand history, the library is a better bet than the local hippy store." He winks at me, and I feel like an absolute fool. Face flaming, I wrench open the car door and get into the driver's seat. He shuts it behind me. Even though I'm not looking at him, I can sense his amusement, and it makes me furious.

"Fine," I say, with both hands on the steering wheel, not looking at him. "Laugh if you want. But those guys at the party didn't wrap their car around a tree without your help. And there's no way all of them got some kind of group concussion that made them forget who I was." I glare at him and have the satisfaction of seeing his smile fade. "You had a bottle smashed over your head," I go on, my voice low and angry, "but you don't have a single scratch. You move as fast on foot as I do in a car. And nearly three centuries ago, your family was given some kind of magic in a totem that you have tattooed on your back. A totem that is supposed to protect people from whatever it is that you've got hidden in my cellar. Am I getting any closer?"

He looks meditatively at me. "You think you've got it all worked out, don't you, Harper?"

"Why are the cellar doors cemented closed?"

His face tightens. "Don't go looking down there for more answers. You won't find anything that makes sense to you."

"You say you're trying to keep me safe." I shake my head in exasperation. "But I'm literally living above whatever it is that's dangerous, and you won't tell me what I can do to protect myself."

"I have told you." He is no longer pretending amusement. Antoine's eyes glitter and his mouth is a hard line. "Sell the house and walk away. That's it, Harper. That's the only thing you can do."

"And what am I supposed to tell my brother? That I have to sell his dream because some woman who doesn't exist is whispering to me from behind a steel door at the end of a secret passage?"

The next moment he's gripping the car door and leaning in, his face grim and furious. "Tell me you didn't go down there."

"Of course I went down there!" I'm so frustrated I could scream. "You knew I could hear her. It's her, the face I drew, isn't it? That I can hear whispering to me?"

His fingers are clenched, and I could swear the metal is actually buckling under his grip. He looks down and lets go abruptly, as if he has just realized the same thing. I stare at the place where his hand just was. There is a clear imprint of his fingers, pressed into the metal as neatly as if it had been done in a factory.

My heart trips, time seeming to slow around me. I can't make immediate sense of what that imprint means, only that it confirms that I'm not crazy. Antoine Marigny is more than whatever facade he presents to the world. Those imprints are hard proof.

"It's nothing, huh?" I raise my eyes to his. I'm not sure what I expect, but when he just stares at me grimly, I turn the key in the engine. "I don't have time for this." I put the car into reverse, too upset and angry to listen to anymore lies.

"Wait." There's something about the way he says it, an edge of raw emotion, that makes me pause. "The kidney you gave your sister. Tessa."

Somehow the fact that he remembers her name touches me. My knuckles grip the steering wheel. I don't answer him, but I don't drive away, either.

"It didn't save her." He says it as a statement, not a question.

"No." My heart twists. "There was never a good chance it would."

"Did she want you to donate it?"

I swallow. "No. She didn't."

"But you did it anyway."

"Yes."

He nods slowly. He looks down at the imprint of his fingers, then back at me.

"Giving you answers," he says quietly, "is like that kidney. It won't help. It won't be a cure for what is wrong. It's the kind of knowledge that will only bring pain, and I think you've already had enough of that in your life. I don't want to give you more."

"That's not your choice to make. Nobody else gets to choose what somebody can or can't handle." I stare down the empty street, remembering Tessa's pale, scared face, Connor's silent desperation. "I'd do it again, for Tessa," I whisper. "I'd make the same decision in a heartbeat."

His eyes search mine. I feel as if he sees inside me, to the time I sat in a hospital room knowing that whatever fear I felt was infinitely preferable to spending the rest of my life wondering *what if.*

Finally he nods, a resigned, brief gesture. "I'll tell you what you want to know. All I ask is that you wait until Monday afternoon. Will you do that?"

I study his face. "Will you still be here on Monday?"

He nods. "I promise."

"And you'll answer any questions I have? Anything at all?"

"You have my word."

"And in the meantime," I say, "Are my brother and I safe?"

"So long as you don't go anywhere near that cellar. And you must promise me not to, Harper. Please."

I drum my fingers on the steering wheel. "Okay," I say finally. "It's a deal. But on Monday, if you aren't waiting for me after school is out, I'm going straight home and knocking in that door, even if I have to buy a jackhammer to do it."

CHAPTER 13

ANTEBELLUM

I can't bear the idea of two more sleepless nights in the mansion, but I also can't bear the thought of Connor being there alone, even though he hasn't had the same dreams I have. I find him in the hardware store and wait until he's done.

"I was thinking," I say. "Without power or water, there isn't a whole lot of work you can do, and neither are going to be connected until Monday, at least." He starts to protest, and I hold up a hand. "Wait. I was thinking we could maybe play hooky, just until Monday morning. You're hoping to win the contract to do antebellum restoration all along the historic trail, right? Well, this morning I was in the historical society, and I found this." I hold up a book I'd bought on my way out. "It's got the histories of all the original mansions, along with their floorplans, and primary accounts from people who stayed in them in their heyday. I was thinking we could drive down the river and stop in each one, starting this afternoon. We could stay overnight in a bed and breakfast on the way, spend tomorrow night in Baton Rouge, then drive back up early Monday in time for school."

Connor's already shaking his head. "I'm trying to organize equipment to get into the cellar tomorrow."

My pulse leaps and I struggle to keep a level expression. I need to

70

put a stop to this, right away. "I know it sounds lame." I grasp at the first thing I think of. "But I'm really missing Mom and Tessa. I was hoping we could go to Baton Rouge, visit their memorial. I know we said we'd make a clean break. I just feel like I didn't say goodbye properly."

It's a low blow, and I inwardly wince at the deception, but it's also the one thing that works.

"Of course." Connor's face softens immediately. "I'd like to visit, too."

In the end, Avery and Cass decide to come as well, to do some shopping. I suspect, looking at Avery's face when she lays eyes on Connor, that she's driven by a little more than shopping, but I figure that if it means keeping my brother from digging up a three-century-old curse, I can live with it.

By the time we get packed and on the way, we only have time to look at two mansions before pulling up at a stately old guesthouse that Cass's mom recommended. Connor pulls his big brother act, and to Avery's clear disappointment, sends us all to bed early, which given how exhausted I am, is actually perfect. The next day I wake up after my first full night's sleep in what feels like forever, and we leave early.

Poking around the old mansions is actually a lot more interesting than I imagined. It also has the added bonus of taking my mind off Antoine Marigny and the way I feel when he's near me, not to mention whatever secret he's hiding.

Connor is so excited that for once he can't get his words out fast enough, which doesn't seem to bother Avery at all, by the way she hangs on every one of them. Cass and I wander around behind them, often just idling in the overgrown gardens beneath grand old trees.

"Mom said you came to see her at the shop," Cass says when we are alone. It's an idyllic afternoon and we're sitting against an enormous oak. "She said you seemed pretty upset about the story behind the mansion."

"Wouldn't you be?" I throw the piece of grass I'm toying with across the ground and pluck another one.

"I don't know." Cass tilts her head consideringly. "You're from the city, so maybe it seems bad to you. But around Deepwater—this whole area, really—every house has a story. A ghost, a murder, a scandal, a witch. Literally every building has some scandalous event attached to it."

"And that doesn't bother anyone?" It's hard to keep the incredulity from my face. "I can't imagine anyone being happy to live in a house with a curse or a ghost."

Or other supernatural creatures who walk around pretending to be normal. I pick up a leaf and shred it with particular force.

"Well, maybe." Thankfully Cass doesn't catch my violent leaf tearing. "But if everyone panicked over the stories, we'd all have to move. I guess you just get used to it. And besides, the stories about the Marigny mansion are pretty cool, when you think about it."

"Pretty cool?" Now I look at her in open amazement. "How on earth are they cool?"

"Well, you know. All the vampire stuff. I mean, vampire pop culture is so hot these days it's a wonder half the girls at school aren't hitting you up for an invitation to your house just on the off chance they might get bitten." She laughs, but it fades away when she sees my face. "Oh," she says, grimacing. "I gather Mom left that part out."

"Uh—yeah. She did." I use sarcasm to hide my shock. "Vampires." I put my head back and roll my eyes. "Perfect."

Except that my heart is now going faster than a trip-hammer.

"It's just—"

"Stories." I use cynicism in an attempt to disguise the tremor in my voice. "Yeah, I know." Seeing how crestfallen she is, I try a smile. "So, what about vampires, then?" I turn my attention to studiously tearing another leaf. "How do they fit into all this?"

"Are you sure you want me to tell you?" I wave the leaf airily, and she continues. "Well, tell me to stop if you get uncomfortable." I choke back a laugh. Uncomfortable really doesn't begin to explain how I feel. "The old stories mention a sickness among the slaves, but Mom's family legends don't call it a sickness. They say the bodies were drained and had bites all over them. And they say the demons were incredibly fast and had unnatural strength."

"Really?" I look at her. "That's it? Has there ever been an imaginary monster that wasn't strong or fast?"

Who are you trying to convince, Harper? I toss the crumbled leaf to the wind and pick up another. Despite my best efforts, I see Antoine Marigny appearing in the street, the imprints in the car door. *Incredibly fast. Unnatural strength.*

"Well, there's more," Cass says defensively. "The stories also say that the demons could enchant people, make them do their bidding, as if they were in a trance. That's one of the reasons they were so dangerous—they could control people's minds. And—" she holds up a triumphant finger "—all the stories say the demons couldn't go out in the sunlight without special things to protect them."

I remember Antoine's burnished brown skin, the way the sun catches his eyes. I can't imagine anyone less afraid of the daylight than him. *Ridiculous.*

But is it?

Unwillingly, my mind begins to throw random things at me. The bottle smashed on his head that left no trace. The men at the lumberyard. *Enchant people....as if they were in a trance.*

Even so. There could be any number of reasons for the men's collective memory loss, the most likely being that Antoine Marigny, in typically arrogant fashion, had bought them off. And anyway—the demons, or whatever they were, had been sealed beneath my house. That I *do* believe, if my dreams are anything to go by.

"So I'm living in a house that has vampires locked away in my cellar?"

Clearly relieved by my light tone, Cass wags a finger at me. "Not just locked away in the cellar. People say that the Marignys themselves became vampires. That's why they all left. And why it was the poor relations who wound up owning the mansion."

"Now that makes absolutely no sense. If all the Marignys were vampires, why would they trap their own kind in the cellar? And if you were going to live forever, wouldn't you take care of your house?"

"You are far too logical." Cass shakes her head in mock annoyance. "How do you ever hope to fit in if you make fun of all our ghost stories? Tourism around here runs on Southern Gothic, you know! Show some respect." Chattering away merrily, Cass goes on to fill me in on some of the other elaborate tales about local mansions.

But I'm no longer listening at all. My own words are echoing inside my head: *If you were going to live forever, wouldn't you take care of your house?*

I sit beneath the tree as Cass carries on talking, the words turning over and over in my mind, putting together pieces so disturbing I almost miss it when Connor says it's time to leave.

CHAPTER 14

ANSWERS

*T*he rest of the journey passes in a blur. Even our visit to Tessa and Mom's memorial plaque is muted, as if something has pushed pause on my emotions. The red magnolia I planted over their combined ashes has grown as tall as me. I'm glad I insisted we planted it, even if it was hard to come by. It's only when Avery and Cass look at the dates on the plaque and then at me that I realize I've never told them about Tessa.

"I knew your mom died and that your father wasn't around," says Avery, reaching for my hand. "But I never knew about your sister."

"They were twins." It's Connor who says it, and I'm grateful, because paused emotions or not, I don't think I could have got those words out. "Tessa was born with a birth defect that affected her kidneys." He glances sideways at me and I nod that it's OK for him to tell them. "Tessa got very sick and both of her kidneys failed. Because they were twins, Harper was a match, and so she donated a kidney. Unfortunately, the kidney became infected."

"Oh, Harper." Cass reaches for the hand Avery isn't holding. "I'm so sorry."

Despite everything that's going on, and the fact that my entire world seems to have turned upside down, it's oddly comforting to have them there, particularly when I see Cass slip her other hand into Connor's. "You lost her too," she murmurs, and instead of pulling away as Connor usually does when Tessa is mentioned, he just stands there, and lets Cass hold his hand.

I stare at the plaque until it blurs in front of my eyes. I've never felt like Tessa lives here. Even though she died before we bought the Marigny mansion, oddly it is there I feel her presence, in the sultry river breeze and soft scent of magnolias. This place simply reminds me of a life I'm glad to have left behind, a time of pain and loneliness. Without Mom and Tessa, Baton Rouge is just another soulless city. This visit feels like a final goodbye.

Sunday night in Baton Rouge, I fall into another deep, dreamless sleep, as if my mind needs to take a break. We leave before dawn and drive back in a sleepy silence, Connor sipping coffee and the rest of us snoozing all the way.

I feel as if I'm wading through a fog, toward a destination I can't quite see. Everything feels slightly unreal, even the passing of time. I know there are things I don't understand. But every time I try to make sense of them, the fog descends again, hiding a truth I'm not sure I want to find. I know Antoine will meet me after school. I'm not certain if I'm looking forward to hearing his story, or if I wish it would just fade into the fog, enchanting me as it goes so I remember none of this.

I make it through classes by pretending to care about them. Jeremiah comes to English class but takes a vacant desk as far away from me as possible. I try to catch his eye, but he studiously ignores me, and when I go to speak to him after class, he looks right at me and scowls with so much dislike I'm taken aback. He pushes rudely past me and strides away down the corridor without looking back.

Trying to make sense of his hostility, I think back to the last time we saw each other. The kegger at Perdu feels like it was an age ago, though it's only been three days. Jeremiah helped me then, stepping in between the bayou men and me. He encouraged me to hear Antoine out rather than judging him. It makes no sense that he'd now be angry about Antoine's and my discussion this afternoon. That's if Antoine has even told him about it. I can't really imagine Antoine as the sharing type.

I add Jeremiah's obvious anger to the long list of things I don't understand.

By the time the end of the day arrives, I feel torn between dread and relief that I will, at last, have some answers.

I don't see Antoine when I first come out of class. It's only when I reach the lot that I realize he is actually underneath my Mustang, screwing something into place. I stare down at the denim-clad legs and hold my books close to my chest. "What are you doing?"

"I told you. Your Mustang has an oil leak." He slides out from underneath the car and I try not to stare at where his shirt rides up, revealing a chiseled torso that will likely add to the many things keeping me awake at night. "Had," he amends, wiping his hands on a corner of his shirt. "It is now fixed, and I can listen to you drive without wincing in sympathy."

I stare at him in astonishment. "We're about to have a conversation about a centuries-old curse, and you choose this moment to fix my car?"

"I was worried I might not have another chance after today. And it would pain me to leave town knowing it was faulty." He gives me a wry smile and gestures to his truck. "Shall we?"

"I'll drive myself." I hug my books even closer to my chest. I don't like the idea of being stuck somewhere alone with him if this conversation ends badly. He raises his eyebrows as if he knows exactly what I'm thinking.

"Fair enough. Your place, then?" I nod. Connor will be working late anyway. Antoine waits for me to pull out, then follows me all the way home, while I practice what I'm going to say. When we arrive, he follows me onto the porch then pauses outside the door. "It might be better if we talk here."

"Okay." I pause, unsure if I should offer him a drink. There's hardly an etiquette for such a situation. He solves it by leaning up against the Ionic column by the porch stairs, as supple and effortlessly elegant as ever, so brown, strong, and vital that every one of my strange thoughts of the past days seems utterly ridiculous. I sit on a bench by the wall, facing him.

"Why don't you start by asking me a question," he says, "and I'll answer it."

I'm poised on a precipice, frightened to leap, yet unable to remain on the edge. I take a deep breath and jump.

"Fine." I look him directly in the eye. "What is hidden in our cellar?"

Part of me expects him to offer yet more half-truths.

"Two bodies." His tone is quiet and matter of fact, and his eyes don't waver from my face. "A woman named Keziah and a man named Caleb."

I swallow my shock.

"Those names sound . . . old." I'm so taken aback by his response it's the only coherent thought I have.

"Keziah and Caleb were very old. They posed as slaves, but they weren't."

"What were they?"

"Ah." He tilts his head to one side. "That is where the story becomes rather complex."

I take a deep breath. "Were they vampires?"

He doesn't move, but his eyes are shuttered and have turned the hard-slate color that I'm learning means I have touched dangerous ground.

"Yes. And then again—no." Seeing the frown forming on my forehead, he says, "Vampires can be killed. A stake in the heart, for example. Fire. Sunlight."

"You seem to know a lot about it."

"Is that a question?" He raises his eyebrows pointedly. After a pause, I shake my head. "Harper," he says quietly, "from here, there is no going back. Do you understand? You're about to go down a path that is dark and dangerous. Before you do, I want you to hear me very carefully: you can still sell this house and walk away from it. Take the money I'm offering you and go, literally anywhere but here. You have just had a glimpse of where this story is going. Before I say another word, think carefully about whether or not you wish to follow it to the end."

I look away from him. At the end of the porch, a white swing hangs from the roof, bright among the faded timbers, robust and strong, fallen petals from the red magnolia lying on it in splashes of crimson. I think of Connor sitting on it drinking his beer on our first night here, the contentment on his face as he said, "We're going to have a better life, Harper."

"Tell me," I say, the memory twisting my heart. "Just tell me the truth."

Antoine crosses his long legs at the ankle and drops his head for a moment, as if feeling the weight of what he is about to say. But when he raises his eyes again, they are detached and remote, his voice taking on a narrator's neutrality.

"The story begins in 1731," he says. He pauses, gauging my reaction, then continues. "Antoine Jacques Marigny was a French plantation owner, one of the very first in this part of Mississippi. It was rumored that he was the disgraced younger son of a French aristocrat, who had fled his homeland after his indiscretions had become too dark for his family to conceal. Either way, he was a savage master, feared by his slaves. But then he took in two guests, and the savagery worsened.

"The newcomers looked like slaves themselves, with features not dissimilar to those who had come from islands around the Caribbean, but they dressed in finery to rival the master himself and dined with the family as equals. The woman was extraordinarily beautiful. Antoine Marigny seemed to be under her spell, as did his sons.

"When the first bodies drained of blood began to appear, there were those among the slaves who knew what they were, who had known such creatures before. These slaves laid in wait, and tried to kill Keziah and Caleb as legend taught: by stake, fire, and sunlight. But though the bodies would fall, and their fires burned the creatures to ash, the pair could not be truly killed. They would rise again, untouched, within the day. And though they preferred the night, Keziah and Caleb walked unaffected in the sun. When Antoine Marigny did not seem concerned by such dark magic, the slaves grew truly afraid."

"But why would the family have entertained them? Surely they suspected what they were?"

I can't bring myself to say Antoine's name, as if to do so will break the spell of his story.

"To answer your first question: at first, I believe the family may have been compelled. The creatures had the power to bend the human mind to their will. As to your second question: after a time, I believe they were so entranced they no longer cared what the creatures were." His eyes are so dark I feel like they've swallowed the light. "Some of the Marigny family fled when they realized what had come amongst them. But Antoine Marigny, with his wife, daughter, and two of his three sons, stayed. Antoine saw in their dark guests an opportunity for advantage, in a place where a man needed every advantage he could get. He thought he and his family would live forever, be invincible. His wife and daughter, though, feared the creatures. His wife descended into madness, her daughter remaining to care for her.

"Antoine and his sons didn't care. They drank the blood of the creatures, and it made them stronger than other men, faster, more intelligent. But it also made them more dangerous, more cruel than they'd ever been—and Antoine Marigny had been both dangerous and cruel long before he or his two sons drank the blood." His face twists with distaste. "The plantation became an orgy of blood and violence. The slaves could not complain, for who would listen? The other masters would not interfere between one of their own and his property. But one day, Keziah and Caleb were stupid enough to go beyond their own lands and into those of the Natchez people. They killed many and took others—women—for their own enjoyment. That was their mistake. And their downfall."

I'm gripped by his story, unable to do anything but simply listen.

"The Natchez chief was called the Great Sun. His wife, Atsila, was the most powerful medicine woman of the tribe, the descendant of another Great Sun. She knew magic the slaves did not, ancient secrets of sun worship that ruled the land.

"In retaliation for what Caleb and Keziah had done, the Natchez captured the men of the Marigny family and gave them an ultimatum: if they helped the Natchez capture the creatures, they would be offered magic just as powerful as that of the creatures' blood and be allowed to use it to make the plantation a success. But if they declined, the Natchez said, the Marigny family would be destroyed." His voice has changed, become slower and more pained, and when he continues, I realize he is no longer seeing me at all. "The Marigny family did a terrible thing. They signed the truce with the Natchez—but then they betrayed it. They went to Keziah and Caleb and told them what the Natchez planned. That night, the creatures turned on slaves and Natchez alike, mad with fury and revenge. They burned the slave quarters and the Natchez village in which lived the Great Sun—only Atsila and a handful of others survived. They burned the fields and the woods, leaving only the mansion standing amid the destruction. The Natchez, who had done all they could to make peace, were left with no choice but to wield their most powerful magic to protect their land and people.

"The Natchez made an alliance with Samuel, one of the slaves who knew blood magic. They hoped that their own link to the land, combined with Samuel's blood magic, could limit the creatures' power and hold them to a single place. But in order to truly contain the creatures inside a house, a place of white man's creation, the Natchez knew they needed a third element—white man's magic. The magic contained on parchment, written in pen and ink. Neither slave nor Natchez were permitted to own land or title. To bind the creatures to the mansion itself, they needed the blood of the white man who did.

"The Natchez hunted down Antoine Marigny's eldest son, who had fled after Keziah and Caleb's arrival. They convinced him to return. Then they used his blood to bind the house forever to the Marigny name on the deed.

"The Natchez attacked. They drove Keziah and Caleb indoors, beneath the house. The Natchez magic flowed between sun and earth, and their ability to wield it was weakened once the creatures were inside a house built and owned by white men.

"It was then that Samuel intervened, weaving blood magic with that of the Natchez to bind the two creatures in place. Finally, the door was sealed, and with it, the final part of the binding, the magic on the deed, came into effect. Antoine Marigny and his younger sons were destroyed, but his wife and daughter lived on. The Marigny Will ensured that the mansion would stay in the family, whether inherited by woman or man. So long as the house was owned by a living holder of the Marigny name, by marriage or descent, connected to the blood dripped onto that deed, the binding would remain strong. But should the house ever pass outside of the family, the binding would be released, and the creatures within able to be freed. There were Natchez who swore to protect the binding, just as Samuel swore on behalf of his people. As the deed holders, the Marigny family became the keeper of the binding, the anchor to which the magic was tied. But the Natchez were not destined to last long under French rule. Soon enough, the binding was the sole burden of the Marigny family."

When his eyes find mine, they are hollow, burned out, full of pain. "That is what lies beneath your house," he says simply. "Two of the most dangerous and bloodthirsty creatures the world has ever known. They are not dead, Harper. They cannot be killed. They are . . . dormant. They need only blood to bring them back to life. They cannot seek it whilst they are still bound in the cellar, and so long as the doors that were blood-sealed stay closed, they can't escape. Before, the door simply couldn't be opened. Now that the binding is broken, there is no magic stopping someone from opening it, and nothing to stop Keziah and Caleb from leaving once they have drunk blood to regain their strength."

My fingers are gripping the bench seat tightly enough to leave marks. The old wood feels like an anchor of normalcy. "And the dreams?" My voice sounds hoarse to my own ears.

"The dreams are Keziah's trick. She has used it across the ages, on the women who have inhabited the house." His face twists. "You might have heard the tales of madness in the Marigny family. They are not rumors, nor are they exaggerated. Keziah whispers to those in the house, particularly women. She pleads with them. More than one has gone mad trying to drown out her voice."

He watches me in silence. I stare at my Mustang, wishing I could get in it and drive away from all of this, leave it behind forever. But I know I can't. Maybe I knew it the day Connor and I first left Baton Rouge and told each other we'd make a new life, one free of grief and pain. *Maybe I knew even then that we couldn't outrun our destiny.*

And besides, I asked for this. Insisted on it. Just like the kidney that I gave Tessa, I cannot take it back simply because I don't like the outcome.

I force myself to let go of the bench and meet his eyes with my own. "When you first asked me to sell the house back to Jeremiah, all I heard was the stuff about the curse. Even later, when it became obvious there was something very wrong, I didn't think about the fact that it was *Jeremiah's* name on those papers. Even when Selena told me about your family history—still, I didn't make the connection." He is watching me intently, but he doesn't say anything. "Then yesterday, I remembered something she said: that the binding only remains in place if the deed is in the name of a living Marigny." I hold his eyes. "A *living* Marigny," I repeat softly.

Still he doesn't move.

"You could have just bought the house yourself. You have the money to ensure it is kept in perpetuity, even restored to its former glory. But you didn't." His fists clench and the muscles in his forearms cord with tension. His eyes are burning dark holes, his every nerve intent upon my face.

"You didn't buy it because you can't." I look at him squarely. "Because you know that if you put your name on that deed, the binding will fall away, and Keziah and Caleb will be released."

"Why?" His voice is low and tense, and he casts the word at me like a weapon. "Tell me why, Harper. Why can't I put my name on the deed?"

I stare at him. "Because you're not living." He waits, reading my face, his eyes urging me to finish the sentence. I close my eyes, then open them again and look right at him.

"Because you're a vampire," I say.

CHAPTER 15

TRUTH

ou're a vampire.

The words are like stones skipping across the river, bouncing in the still afternoon light then sinking beneath the surface. I can't sit still anymore. Coming to my feet, I move restlessly down the porch, my back to him. When I turn around, he's still leaning against the column, watching me, motionless as a statue.

"How old are you?" Of all the questions I could ask, it seems the easiest.

"I was twenty-three when I became what I am."

From nowhere, I have the thought that Connor wouldn't like the idea of me dating someone six years older than me. Then I wonder where the idea of dating entered my mental conversation. A moment after that, I realize that I'm talking about Antoine being a *vampire* and think that both the issue of dating and the age gap are more than a little irrelevant. I can feel his eyes on me, but I don't have it in me to ask any questions right now.

"I drink blood to survive, just as Keziah and Caleb did." I'm oddly grateful that he volunteered that information without my having to ask. "I can eat or drink anything you can, but my body doesn't need it and isn't nourished by it."

LUCY HOLDEN

I'm not sure what I expected. Perhaps that maddening half smile of his, an amused laugh at the mere idea of him being a vampire. Maybe flat, hard denial, the slate-gray stare and grim mouth. Even, perhaps, a rude rejoinder and abrupt exit.

But not this bland, simple statement of fact, the mundanities of what he is rather than an acknowledgement of the sheer insanity of it. It's like someone taking me to the moon and then explaining the rocket ship's inner workings. And most overwhelming of all is the fact that this is *Antoine*, the burnished bronze man with a touch that makes me shiver and whose face, whether I like it or not, haunts my waking hours almost as much as Keziah does my sleeping ones.

His eyes are dark, unreadable. I want to see behind them to whatever danger lurks within, as if by doing so I will know if he can hurt me. I wonder why I'm asking the question, given all he's just said.

Antoine is a vampire. Of course he's dangerous.

The simple reality is that he could kill me right now, and I'd barely have a moment to so much as think about fighting back. The only reason he hasn't, I think dully, is because I still serve a purpose.

Not because of any other reason.

I wonder why that should make me sad.

"Who inherited the mansion after you—" I gesture, unable to say the word *died*. It seems impossible that a man who radiates so much life could be dead.

"My sister. The women of the Marigny line are famous these days for retaining their own name after marriage. It was forgiven as a quirk of an old, aristocratic French family."

"What I don't understand," I say, "is why, if you are able to 'compel' the minds of others, as you put it, you haven't simply compelled me to sell the house?"

"I tried."

"You don't deny it, then." My hands ball into fists at my side. I find myself searching for a reason to get angry. I want to react somehow, to find something around which to pivot emotions too tumultuous to make sense of.

"Did you really expect me to deny it?" He doesn't wait for me to answer. "I did try to compel you. That first day, on the dock, when I told you that you should sign the papers." He's watching me sift through the conversation in my mind. "You asked if that approach usually works for me. Do you remember?"

Does that usually work for you? Turning up at a stranger's house at dusk and just ordering them to do what you want?

"You told me that I should rethink my decision."

He nods. "And I told you that my approach generally does work." His lips twitch. A glimmer of amusement hovers behind the dark eyes and despite everything, I feel glad to see it, and that makes me angry all over again.

"Then why didn't it work on me?"

There's a moment when I think I can see uncertainty behind his eyes, but he sounds sure enough when he answers. "It's because your name is on the deed. I think it makes you part of the magic in a different way than the Marignys who have lived here over the years. The owner of the mansion is normally immune to the dreams, although other family members have often been driven mad by the visions of Keziah and the sound of her voice. Normally, the owner is both bound by the curse and governed by it. If they were reluctant to comply, I could always compel them if necessary." His mouth twists wryly. "Though I rarely needed to."

"Then how is it different for me?"

His smile fades. "You don't have the protection of the Marigny name—or the magic that binds us to the land and house. Which means that Keziah is free to compel you, to place her own control over your mind. Even weakened as she is, Keziah possesses unusual power. I imagine that she is blocking my ability to compel you, seeking to bend you to her will." He pushes off from the porch and is suddenly standing directly in front of me, his eyes searching mine. "Have you found yourself drawn toward the sound of her voice? Compelled to go to her?"

I think of the night I went into the library, following the secret passage downstairs, following her whispers. He sees it in my eyes and nods. "I thought so. She can feel the curse is gone. Before, she could torment the residents of the house, harangue them—but not control them. You, however, are a different matter. It's astonishing that you've managed to resist her this long." He brushes a stray curl of hair from my cheek, and I look up, startled, to find him watching me, some emotion I can't quite read shifting behind his eyes. He steps back abruptly. "You can see why it's imperative to get you out of here as quickly as possible." The warmth of a moment ago is gone, his tone hard once more. "If Keziah can compel your mind, it's only a matter of time until she forces you to release her. To be frank, I'm surprised she hasn't tried before now."

I don't think it's wise to mention that she already has. Instead, I say, "If I sell the house back to Jeremiah, and the deed is transferred back into the Marigny name, Keziah will be bound once more?"

He nods. "The door to the cellar remains blood-sealed. So long as it remains closed, nothing can enter or leave the cellar. But your name on the deed has weakened the actual magic in the earth. Keziah is strong, and she is old. She will have sensed the change. Her powers of mind control will continue to grow. If by any chance the door is opened, the binding will not be strong enough to hold her to the Marigny land. Even with a Marigny name on the deed, it would take Natchez blood to close the door and seal it again. But if the Marigny name goes back on the deed before that door is opened, the binding will return to its former strength, making the owner immune to Keziah's whispers, though other residents of the house are not."

"You sound very certain."

He tilted his head. "I've done my homework."

"Is that where you were, the last two days? Doing your homework?"

"That. And—other things." He looks at me and sighs. "I know that after this conversation, my time in Deepwater will be brief. I wanted to organize everything I needed so that I can leave as soon as we've fixed this."

"You're leaving?" The words are out before I can catch them. His eyes narrow.

"I assumed that is what you would want me to do."

"It is." I stare at him coldly. "And when you're finished 'fixing this,' you'll just leave, and never come back?"

"Not in your lifetime," he says quietly.

"And I won't remember anything about this, will I?" I don't need any help now to feel angry. Frustration rises in a hot tide. "The moment that deed is back in Jeremiah's name, you'll compel me and my brother. We'll have a new mansion for Connor to restore, but he'll lose the grant he won. You can't compel an entire committee or the media who reported it. His reputation, the opportunity for him to win contracts all along the historic trail, to make his dreams come true— all of that will be gone, and we won't even remember why."

"You'll be safe." His face is resigned. He rubs a hand over his jaw and looks away from me.

I stare unseeing at the moss hanging from the live oaks along the driveway. All the information I've learned over the past several days settles in my mind like pieces of a dark jigsaw. I hear Selena's voice in my mind: *The Marignys were sadists. They were known as heartless masters who abused their slaves terribly . . . The Natchez woman captured the magic inside the Marigny boy himself, but it wasn't destroyed. It drove him mad, made him the worst of them all.*

I remember asking her what would happen if the binding was broken.

Then there's nothing left to hold the darkness captive. It's free to escape.

And kill people. Like Jeremiah's parents. My internal response to Selena snaps the last pieces of the jigsaw in place, forming a sickening picture of the extent to which Antoine Marigny will go to guard his dark legacy.

"Don't pretend this is about keeping me safe." My anger is a righteous force now, so strong I can barely look at him. "Jeremiah will be bound to a curse he can't ever break. Connor will lose his dream. Keziah and Caleb will still be down there, not dead, not gone, just waiting for another opportunity like this one. And you will simply ride off in your perfectly restored Chevy to your untouched, immortal life, where nobody knows you're a monster just as bad as the ones you were created to destroy." He doesn't flinch from my words. His impassivity goads me. "You betrayed the people who believed in you. You were supposed to be locked up in that cellar too. That was part of the truce you made with the Natchez, wasn't it? But instead of accepting your prison, you cheated your way to freedom. They say you became a madman, worse than your family had ever been. And now you are about to do the same thing all over again." I shake my head in contempt. "Did you kill Jeremiah's parents to frighten us, Connor and I? Or as revenge? Or just to make people start talking about the curse again?"

My question is met with hard silence and eyes that give nothing away. I wait, unwilling to let the question lie.

"I did become a madman," he says quietly, "worse than my family had ever been. And yes, I should have been locked inside that cellar." He doesn't flinch from my gaze, but I can't see behind the mask covering his own, and after a further moment of silence, I know he won't tell me what I want to know. I'm not sure if that's because he is guilty, or if he simply wants me to believe the worst of him. Either way, I'm frustrated and don't want to hear any more.

"I don't know how Jeremiah can stand the sight of you." I spin away from him and go to the door, then pause on the threshold.

"The stories about vampires needing to be invited in—are they true?"

He nods slowly. "If a human owns the house, then yes, a vampire can't enter without an invitation."

"Well, as the owner of this house, I don't invite you in. I never will." I cross my arms, unsure if I'm saying it for his benefit or my own. "And if you think I'm selling this house to Jeremiah, you can think again." His head jerks up in surprise.

"After everything you've just heard," he says tightly, "you can't be serious, Harper."

"I've never been more serious in my life." I glare at him from the other side of the threshold, holding on to my anger like I had to the wooden bench earlier, as an anchor to keep me steady. "So long as I own this house, you can't compel me to leave it, nor to forget that you are a lying psychopath without a conscience who uses people for his own advantage. You're going to help me find a way to kill your friends in the cellar and destroy whatever darkness infects them. When we've done that, I'm going to hold you to the truce you signed with the Natchez all those years ago, to ensure the curse never harms anyone else. A truce you clearly never had any intention of abiding by. You probably thought the Natchez were no better than the slaves you tortured and killed." I can hear my voice shaking, but I don't care. "Times have changed, Antoine. You aren't a plantation owner anymore, free to use people for your own profit as you see fit. I might not be able to tell people what you are. But I can make sure you never hurt anyone else again—especially not Jeremiah."

His face has grown darker as I speak. By the time I finish, there is no trace of emotion left in his expression, just a cold, ancient stillness that makes me take an involuntary step backward.

"If you remain the owner of this house," he says flatly, "you will die. It may take a week, or a month—but you will die. Keziah and Caleb will escape. And everything you say you want to prevent will happen, only worse, far worse, than you could possibly imagine."

"I know my name can't remain on the deed. I have no intention of letting Keziah, or anyone else, control my mind."

He frowns. One finger taps the column impatiently. "Then what, exactly, do you plan to do, Harper? You can't transfer it to your brother. If you sell it, you condemn someone else to your own fate, and somehow, I doubt you will do that."

A red magnolia flower drifts down to lie on the wooden boards of the porch, its soft, fragrant petals in painful contrast to the hard tension between us. I raise my eyes from it back to Antoine.

"You're going to marry me." I stare straight at him. "And give me the Marigny name."

CHAPTER 16

SOLUTION

"*M*arry you?" Antoine is staring at me in complete disbelief. "I can't marry you."

"Yes, you can." Now that I've made up my mind, it all seems very clear. "We'll drive to Jackson on Wednesday."

He blinks dazedly. "You're underage."

"And you're a vampire." I stare him down. "It's legal for minors to marry in Mississippi with parental consent. You will compel a judge to sign the consent form and any other official to do what they need to." I raise my eyebrows and look at him pointedly. "It's not like you haven't already compelled half the officials in town to stop the water and power from being put on. Oh, wait." I look skyward, as if I've just had an epiphany. "I think they've just realized their oversight and feel a sudden urge to get the Marigny mansion connected as their utmost priority." I cock my head and fold my arms. "I expect to be having a hot shower, with the lights on, tomorrow."

"You can't marry me."

"Did you hear what I just said about the water and power?" I'm starting to take a savage satisfaction in seeing his customary composure so ruffled.

"There's no guarantee it will even work."

"Yes, it will. The curse requires the name of a Marigny, by marriage or descent. I'm definitely alive, and after Wednesday, I'll be a Marigny by marriage. You compel the right officials, we change the name on the deed, and voilà." I snap my fingers. "Done."

"It's the most ridiculous idea I've ever heard." He steps closer to the door, as if he'd like nothing more than to reach out and strangle me. I stand just over the threshold with my arms crossed and smile sweetly. He plants one hand high on either side of the doorframe and eyes me with what he no doubt considers a menacing look. "What are you planning on telling your brother?"

"Absolutely nothing. And neither will you. Not Jeremiah either. This is between you, me, and the attorney you will compel to change the name on the title of the house."

"Jeremiah." He pounces on the name with satisfaction. "If you're intent upon doing something so insane, you can marry him."

"No." I drop my light tone and meet his eyes steadily. "You've done more than enough to ruin Jeremiah's life. He's lost his parents and probably most of his sanity. I won't put him through any more. I want him free of this house and the curse upon it." I pause, my eyes narrowing. "And while we're on the topic—when this is over, and you leave Deepwater for good, you won't ever come near Jeremiah again. Not ever. Do you understand?" I remember Jeremiah's earlier anger and wince. *No wonder he loathes me.* He's already lost his parents. Now he has a vampire as a guardian and is caught in a trap only I can free him from.

Antoine is still gripping the doorframe above me, so hard I can almost hear the timber creaking, his face grim as he stares at me. I stare right back. Finally, his head drops down, shaking in exasperation. "This is ridiculous," he mutters again.

"But you'll do it," I say flatly. "You don't have a choice. You can't compel me to go, and if the title stays in my maiden name, it's only a matter of time until Keziah compels me to release her, as you said. This is the only way, and you know it." He shakes the doorframe and pushes back, pacing the porch agitatedly.

"Why do you want this?" He flings the words at me with palpable frustration. In contrast to his earlier composure he's restless, unable to stand still. His eyes glitter with a strange, fierce light. "Even if we were of the same time, I would still be six years older than you."

"Given the centuries between us, not to mention the reason for the marriage, I don't see the relevance."

"You don't see the *relevance?*" He stops pacing and rakes a frustrated hand through his hair. "Marriage is—it isn't something to take lightly."

"Neither is my brother's dream. Or the future we've planned together." I meet his frustration with anger of my own.

"You're risking your life. Your brother's life. All because Connor won a grant to fix this house?"

"Connor chose this house. He drove up here from Baton Rouge and went through every ruin along the historic trail. He worked construction by day, and at night he'd sit up until his eyes crossed, drawing and redrawing the plans." I shake my head, remembering the dark days when Tessa was sick, the days following her death. "Don't talk to me about what I do or don't take lightly. My entire life has been lived in death's shadow. Do you think that age defines that experience?"

Antoine stops pacing and looks at me with that disquieting scrutiny that always makes me feel as if I'm under a magnifying glass. When he doesn't interrupt, I go on, giving voice to things I've thought, but never openly said to anyone. "Tessa, Connor, and I were all forced to grow up long before we were ready. We learned to make hard decisions—and then stand by them. All Connor has ever wanted is to be an architect. He didn't have to stay after Mom died to look after Tessa and me. Connor isn't even my brother. His father was just some guy my mother lived with when we were young."

"He's not your brother?" Antoine looks surprised. "You have the same name."

"Connor changed it before we moved up here. Neither of us wanted to draw attention to ourselves. He said that Mom was the best parent he'd had anyway, and that Tessa and I were his family, no matter what our names were. He won a scholarship to study architecture at Louisiana State, but when Mom got sick with cancer, he left college and moved back in to help, studying at night. When Tessa got sick a year later, he worked three jobs to pay for medical bills until Mom's insurance money came through. He took me to school and made sure there was dinner on the table. He sat with Tessa when she was in the hospital and talked to the doctors when they would have dismissed me. Connor is the only reason Tessa and I weren't put into the system. If it weren't for him . . . my life would be a ruin. And then, against all the odds, and despite being an undergrad with no experience, he won a state competition. Based on plans he drew—for *this* house." I look at Antoine. "This mansion is his dream," I say quietly. "A chance for him to leave behind his drunk father and all the things that have gone wrong, to create a new life for himself. I won't take that away from him. No matter what I have to do."

"Even if it means marrying a monster." There's a strange note in Antoine's voice, and when I look up at him he's regarding me with the same expression I remember from the first day we met on the dock, as if I'm a puzzle he can't quite work out.

"Yes," I say. "Even then."

He purses his lips and looks away. When he turns back, he looks resigned. "We'll drive to Jackson on Wednesday." He looks at me sternly. "You'll change the name on the deed the same day." I nod. "In the meantime, you will stay at Avery's house." I start to argue, and he holds up a hand. "That is nonnegotiable. Keziah is too dangerous."

"What do I tell Connor?"

"That the weather is getting colder and you need hot showers. I'll see to it that the power and water are connected." He turns to go down the steps, still shaking his head.

"Wait." He pauses but doesn't turn around.

"What?" I'm pretty sure he's speaking through gritted teeth, and I get a grim satisfaction at seeing his hands stretch, as if he's having to try not to clench them in frustration.

"The moment this is all over," I say, "and the curse is broken, do you promise to leave and never come back? Never bother any of us, including Jeremiah, again?" There's a silence that stretches out. I can feel the tension in my body as I wait for him to speak. Finally, his shoulders seem to fall slightly, and he says in a low voice, "Yes, Harper. If we manage to find a way around the curse, and kill Keziah and Caleb, and if that is what you want—then, yes. I promise to leave. And never come back."

"That is what I want."

"Very well." He walks stiffly to the truck without looking back. I feel a twinge of guilt and am immediately annoyed. *Why on earth should I feel guilty for wanting a sadistic vampire far away from my life and those of the people I care about?* He opens the car door and glances up at where I stand, still just inside the door to the house.

"Until Wednesday, then," he says.

I nod coldly but don't answer. He gets into the Chevy and drives away.

This time, I don't watch him go.

CHAPTER 17

FLOWERS

*T*he moment he's gone, I lurch into a frenzy of activity to prevent me from having to actually think about everything that has just taken place.

I leave a note for Connor saying I'm at Avery's. I know he'd see straight through me if we were face-to-face. After a moment, I add a line to the note saying that I want him to wait until we're together to use equipment to open the cellar. *Better safe than sorry.*

I throw some clothes in a bag then realize that I will need something to get married in.

What is the dress code for a fake wedding to a three-century-old vampire?

I shake my head and rummage around in a box marked FANCY, one of the many I haven't yet unpacked. Tessa used to design and make a lot of our clothes. Some are zany, some so beautiful they seem to come from another time and place. Since she got sick, I haven't worn a stitch she made for me. It just hurts too much. I give up a moment later, realizing I'm still not ready. I wonder if I ever will be.

There doesn't seem to be much point opening boxes of clothes I'll never wear, when there's not even a closet to unpack them into. I find an emerald silk dress I bought to wear to Junior Prom before Tessa got sick. It still has the tag on it. I stuff it into my overnight bag with my other things and pause at the door of my bedroom. Keziah's face stares back at me from my easel. I scowl at it.

Help me.

"Oh, go to hell," I snap out loud.

Avery is very understanding, considering we've just spent two days together and she's probably sick of my face. "You can stay in the spare room as long as you like," she says, after I go through a disjointed ramble about dirty water and bugs. "Are you sure Connor's going to be okay out there on his own?" I'm banking on the fact that so far, he seems to have had no bad dreams and that his name isn't on the deed, when I assure her he is. "I might head out there to see him anyhow," she says. "Take him some cookies or something." I'm willing to bet her desire to feed my brother has very little to do with charity and a whole lot more with the way she was looking at him during our road trip, but I don't comment other than to say that sounds like a nice idea. Who am I to judge?

I'm hoping to have a chat with Jeremiah at school, but the following day he doesn't show up, and I try not to imagine all the horrendous ways Antoine could be taking out his frustration. I reassure myself with the thought that I've made it very clear that Jeremiah is to remain out of the entire mess. Somehow, I don't think Antoine will go against my wishes. Not while the curse is still down, at least.

I push away the other, more disturbing thoughts, that crowd my mind when I think of Antoine being a vampire. Even the word twists in my mind, not seeming quite real. Somehow the image I have of vampires is more suited to Jeremiah than Antoine—thin and pale, tortured looking. Antoine is nothing like that. He's powerful and vital, and when he isn't grim and angry, his eyes are so vivid they seem to pierce the light itself. He seems born to the outdoors rather than the darkness, as if he carries the sun inside him rather than fearing it. I frown as I suddenly realize that I still don't know how he walks around in daylight. There are so many things I forgot to ask him—and so many things I said that I never imagined saying to anyone, let alone him. There is something in his lethal stillness, an intense kind of focus, that seems to draw my innermost feelings to the surface, causing me to confide things I barely even know I feel until they're said. It is a strange intimacy. I've never been the talker in my family, preferring to keep what I feel carefully contained. Soul-baring isn't my style. I'm unsettled by how much I revealed. I keep seeing his face, the way he watched me quietly as I spoke, seeming to absorb every word as if he truly heard it. Heard *me*.

Then I return to the comforting security of anger and chastise myself for imagining Antoine Marigny's piercing eyes and powerful body when I hate everything about him. I remind myself that I want nothing more than for him to leave and never come back, so my life can go back to normal. Well, whatever normal is, in my life.

The problem is that despite all that Selena told me and that he himself confessed, I'm horribly aware that I don't truly hate Antoine.

I find it impossible to reconcile the man with the wicked half smile, who wants to fix the leak in my car, with the madman who tortured slaves and possibly killed Jeremiah's parents. The truth is I simply don't know what to believe. And if I'm perfectly honest with myself . . . I'm as fascinated by Antoine Marigny as I ever was.

I don't like myself very much for that. Somehow I feel as if I should have more moral strength. I've never understood girls who fall for the Bad Boy type. In the little thought I've given it, I've always believed heroes should be firmly cast in the honorable, reliable mold, rather than one of danger. I'm not sure what it says about me that despite all I know of Antoine's past, his eyes still seem to haunt my every waking moment.

Avery bakes cookies that night and tells me she's planning to take them to Connor on Wednesday, which suits me fine. "I'm going to do some stuff for my art project," I tell her. "I'll take my own car. I might be a bit late coming back. There's a spot just out of town I want to try sketching at dusk."

She rolls her eyes and tells me I'm a total art geek, which is fine by me. I get a text just before I go to bed from a strange number with an address and a time, and I realize Antoine must have taken my details from Jeremiah's phone. *You can leave your car at Jeremiah's house,* it reads. *We'll take mine.*

On Wednesday I wait until everyone has left the house before I get dressed. I have a moment when I stare at the clothes laid out on the bed and wonder if I should simply throw them in the trash and show up in jeans and a T-shirt. But some deep, proud part of me rebels at that. I've made a choice, and I will stand by it. But I won't make my wedding vows in jeans, as if this were some midnight Vegas getaway. Regardless of what monster I'm marrying, it is my decision, and I will wear it proudly. Instead I take extra care, piling my hair up in a loose knot that lets curls fall about my face, applying makeup, and wearing the pearl drop earrings Mom left to me. *Something borrowed,* I think, my heart twisting. The emerald silk dress matches my eyes, making them seem larger than normal. I have the strappy heels I originally bought to go with the dress, and when I finally look in the mirror, I feel as if Mom and Tessa wouldn't be ashamed if they saw me.

When I park outside Jeremiah's house, for a moment I suspect I have the wrong address. It's a two-story modern place built of timber and glass, jutting out over the water, with a dock built underneath. It's only when I recognize the boat tied there as the one Antoine drove the day we met that I'm sure I have the right place. It's peaceful and beautiful, surrounded by dogwood and redbud, with cypress in the marshy ground below the house. I'd had the impression that Jeremiah's parents had no money at all. I hadn't realized he'd live in such a nice house. I go to open my car door, hoping I will get a chance to talk to Jeremiah, but as I reach for the handle, Antoine emerges from the house and pulls the front door closed behind him.

I try not to stare.

He's wearing a black suit and white shirt, but that is where any nod to convention ends. The suit jacket is open, as is his shirt at the neck. The contrast between his burnished skin and the fine white cotton is stark. The way the suit trousers hang off his lean frame is a runway model's dream. With his tousled hair and faint stubble shadow, he manages to look brooding, disheveled, and impossibly elegant all at once. He catches me watching him, and his eyes flare slightly. I feel unwelcome color warm my face. I step out of the car to hide my discomfort. When I look back, he hasn't moved at all. He is staring at me, his mouth slightly parted, and his eyes seem to blaze a trail on my skin.

I shrug uneasily. "I didn't really know what to wear," I mutter, then think how ludicrous it is to even think of such things under the circumstances.

"You're stunning." His voice is slightly rough, and he still hasn't moved. When I color even more deeply and reach for my bag, he seems to jolt out of whatever it was and indicates a garage off to the left. "I'll just bring the car out." I glance at the Chevy parked close by, but he presses a button and the garage door goes up, revealing a sleek black Mercedes. "I thought it would be more comfortable," he says, almost apologetically. As he opens the door for me to get in, I feel a sneaking relief that I've made the effort. There's something so darkly magnetic about him in that suit that I know I'd have felt horribly underdressed in anything casual.

He closes the door and I stare straight ahead, unwilling to look at him in case he sees how completely unnerved I am by the entire situation. Getting married to him had seemed like such a perfect, simple idea when I had it. A neat solution to a complex problem that had the added advantage of being guaranteed to annoy the hell out of Antoine himself. But now that I'm sitting in a leather seat beside his silent form, driving up the highway toward the Jackson City Hall, I wonder what on earth I was thinking. I find myself thinking sadly of my mom, and Tessa, and then even more guiltily of Connor.

I mentally shake myself. *This isn't my wedding.* This is a temporary measure that will save Connor and hopefully free Jeremiah from a centuries-old curse. And what is a wedding, anyway? No more than some words on a piece of paper. It isn't like it means anything. Not really.

"I know this isn't real." Antoine is staring straight ahead. His voice is low and, I realize, faintly uncertain. "But I thought that since it is a wedding, after all, you should have flowers." He nods toward the backseat. I swivel around to find a bouquet of dusty miller, dahlias, lavender roses, pink astilbe, and amaranthus, bound together with antique lace. It is wild and unstructured, but somehow utterly perfect.

"It reminded me of you," he says, then breaks off abruptly, as if he's said too much.

"Thank you. It's beautiful."

"I also took the liberty of getting rings." He casts me a brief, sideways glance. "The ceremony will ask for them, and I thought it would be awkward if we didn't have any."

"Of course." It's hard to actively loathe someone when they're being so thoughtful. "You've probably done all this before." I bite my lip, regretting the words as soon as I say them. There's a short pause.

"No, actually," he says quietly. "I haven't." He's still staring ahead and doesn't meet my eyes. Above the collar of his shirt, a pulse beats under his skin, a strange reminder that whatever he has become after death, he still possesses a heart. The thought is oddly comforting. I realize that in his own way, Antoine is as unsure of himself today as I am. The realization is so novel it silences me. I sit back in the seat and turn to look out the window, uncertain why it is that someone so inherently powerful could in the same breath strike me as so extraordinarily vulnerable.

CHAPTER 18

VOWS

We're fifty miles north of Deepwater when Antoine casts me a sideways glance. "May I show you something?"

"What time is our—appointment?" I feel color on my face again. I can't bring myself to say "wedding."

"Not for several hours. We've got plenty of time." When I nod, he turns off down a side road and then through a gate that says Private Property.

"Are you sure we should be here?" I look around nervously, but Antoine just half smiles and keeps driving. The dirt road opens up into a wide, somewhat overgrown field. In the center of it, surrounded by gnarled oaks hung in moss, stands an old, small stone church, with arched windows and turrets. It's enchanting, like a secret castle from a fairy tale. Just by the door a red magnolia blazes in full bloom, despite the lateness of the season. Antoine parks under a tree and we get out. The air is still and quiet and sweet with magnolia scent. The door to the church is open.

"What is this place?" I look around, half expecting to face an irate farmer with a rifle.

"It's an old church. It was built in 1839, on the site of an earlier church built by a friend of mine a century before." Antoine reaches out and touches the warm stone gently, tracing the year that is engraved there. "I always thought it would be—nice—to get married here."

"I can see that." Part of me wants to just stay here, in the welcoming peace offered by the church's open door. When I think of the bustling office at City Hall, I can feel only a dragging sense of dread. I catch hold of myself. This isn't a real wedding, and there's nothing romantic about it. City Hall is exactly the place to make it official, I tell myself firmly. Anything else would be a lie. No matter what internal confusion I might be suffering, this marriage is not one either of us actually asked for, and to pretend otherwise is bordering on dangerous fantasy.

"We should probably go." I turn toward the car, my heart twisting with strange regret. This church is beautiful. If things were different . . . if this wasn't a farce, it would be perfect. I feel as if I'm swimming through an alternate reality. There is the truth I know, where Antoine is a vampire I'm forced to marry to save my home and brother from destruction. And then there is the reality my heart feels, where I'm standing in a sunlit churchyard amid flowers, beside the most stunning man I've ever seen, who seems to understand me in a way nobody ever has.

"Wait." Antoine's hand closes on mine. I feel a faint shock. His eyes have changed, become gentler somehow, his face gleaming in the sunlight. "We could get married here, if you wish."

"Here? How?" I look around, bewildered.

He gestures inside the church and his mouth turns up at the corners. "There's a priest inside," he confides. "I found him yesterday. And I have a license." He taps his pocket, and I'm about to ask how he's managed to acquire a marriage license when I realize the futility of asking a vampire with powers of mind control such a question. Instead I ask, "What exactly would the priest have done if we never showed up?"

"Waited until midafternoon, then decided he'd had a nice day out and gone home." He grins, and I bite my lip and look away. "Careful."

He reaches out and touches my cheek. "You almost looked like you were smiling."

My conscience is telling me to get right back into the car and head straight for Jackson. Spend five dull minutes in a beige office sandwiched between the other couples with a license in hand, then drive home, sign whatever papers I need to, and forget this whole farce ever happened.

Then I look at Antoine, so devastatingly handsome I can barely breathe with him near. His eyes on me are rich with something I don't understand and don't want to think about. His gaze makes me feel powerful and thrilled at the same time, as if I'm stepping off a cliff into an unknown sea of reckless abandonment that is both the most exhilarating thing I can imagine and the most terrifying prospect I've ever faced.

"Well?" His eyes search mine. "What do you want to do, Harper?"

I open the car door and reach for the bouquet. "I'll probably regret this."

"I very much hope you do not." He holds the door open as I stand up.

"Antoine." I stop, frowning, and he looks at me questioningly. "What's your middle name?"

His mouth twists slightly at the corner. "Jacques."

"Mine is Abigail." I bite my lip and glance away. "I just thought it was something we should know. You know, before . . ." I shrug, my words trailing off.

His eyes are dark and unsettling, but his mouth is still slightly curved. "Well," he says quietly. "I'm glad we got that sorted out." He puts his arm out. "Are you ready?" After a moment, I nod. I put my arm through his, and we enter the church.

It smells of magnolias and old wood, and it makes me think of family and history and all the things I've always cared about. We walk over the uneven stone floor, and the priest smiles at us in welcome, behaving for all the world as if our wedding is the most normal thing imaginable.

"Does he have any idea?" I whisper out of the side of my mouth.

"Not a clue." Antoine's eyes sparkle with mischief, and this time I can't prevent a reluctant smile. His own grows wider. "That," he murmurs, "is the most beautiful thing I've seen all day." He smiles down at me in a way that makes my stomach curl, and we face the priest together.

The words roll over me. All I can feel is Antoine's arm under my hand, his lean strength beside me oddly reassuring. When the priest asks for the rings, Antoine reaches into his pocket. Taking my hand, he gently slides a delicate filigree silver ring onto my finger. An exquisitely cut emerald is set in the center, surrounded by tiny diamonds, and when I look up at him, there is something serious in his eyes that makes my heart quicken and my eyes unable to look away.

"In the name of God," he says quietly, "I take you, Harper Abigail Ellory, to be my wife. To have and to hold from this day forward, for better or worse, for richer or poorer, in sickness and in health. To love and to cherish, until we are parted by death. This is my solemn vow."

He hands me the other ring, a plain silver band. Suddenly worried I won't be able to speak, I place it on his finger, the act feeling so intimate it shakes me to the core.

"In the name of God," I say in a slightly unsteady voice, "I take you, Antoine Jacques Marigny, to be my husband. To have and to hold from this day forward, for better or worse, for richer or poorer, in sickness and in health. To love and to cherish, until we are parted by death." I raise my eyes to him on the last word and find him watching me with such intensity I feel the words on my mouth like a caress. "This is my solemn vow," I say softly.

Antoine is holding both of my hands in his, so close I can see every fleck of gold in his eyes and feel the steady pulse of his heart as if it were my own.

"You may kiss the bride," says the priest.

I had planned to touch cheeks, or not kiss him at all, or to not even think about it. But then the words are said and he is there, staring at me, so vital and real, so close, that before I know what I am doing I am swaying forward and my eyes are closing, and then his lips are on mine.

Perhaps it could have been a fleeting thing, a momentary caress that we both pulled away from. It begins that way, a light touch, wondering. But then his hand comes up to cradle my face, I sway into him, and the kiss is no longer fleeting but hot and sweet and full of something that makes my heart clench in longing and my body ache. He smells of cedar and sunlight and feels like molten heat, and the church and the priest fade away until there is only his mouth on mine and the world between us.

When it finally ends, I open my eyes to find him staring at me in a way that makes fire lick through my veins, and the priest beaming at us as if it's the happiest day of our lives.

We sign the register and the priest hands Antoine a certificate. Antoine looks at him. "You may go now," he says, his voice low and commanding. "You were never here. Until I say otherwise, you don't remember marrying us. Say it."

"I can go now." The priest stares at him. "I was never here. I don't remember marrying you."

Antoine draws my arm through his own and we walk out of the darkened church and into the sunlight, joined until death as man and wife, in the sight of God.

CHAPTER 19

BROKEN

*E*verything about the drive back to Deepwater feels like it's happening through a golden haze. Sunlight dapples through the trees on the side of the road. The radio is playing old blues that feel like happier days, and when I lower the window a fraction, the air smells like cypress and magnolias.

We've barely spoken since we left the church. I'm terribly aware of Antoine sprawled in the driver's seat, one hand resting loosely on the wheel, his new wedding ring glinting in the sun. His other hand lies close enough to touch. I'm afraid of how much I want to.

"We should go straight to the clerk's office." Antoine breaks the silence as we near town. His voice is slightly hoarse. His eyes touch my face then look swiftly away, as if he's afraid to look at me too long. "The process of changing your name would normally take weeks, but I should be able to make it happen immediately. You will need to be there, though."

"Sure." I glance down at the emerald glowing among diamonds on my finger. I want to touch it, and I want to give it back to him. I know how wrong this all is. I'm torn between self-contempt and a strange, creeping sense of wonder.

We're married. I'm Harper Marigny now.

"I hope you like it." He looks down at the emerald.

"I'll give it back," I say quickly, reaching for it.

"No." He says it so forcefully I stop mid-gesture. He clears his throat. "That is—wear it or not, as you wish. But it is yours. I would like you to keep it."

"What about you?" My voice is slightly husky. "Will you wear yours?"

We are pulling into the lot outside the clerk's office. He stops the car and meets my eyes directly for the first time since we left the church. "Always," he says, and the word is so loaded with meaning that all I can do is stare at him. He holds my eyes for a long time. Then he gets out and comes around to open my door. He offers me his hand and when I stand up, I am right in front of him, so close my legs touch his, and he is still holding my hand. He gives me a crooked smile and his eyes caress my face in a way that turns my stomach to mush. "Are you ready to do this, Mrs. Marigny?"

He doesn't wait for an answer. He keeps hold of my hand as we go in, and I don't take it away.

In the end, it takes less than half an hour to change my name. I'm aware of Antoine's phone buzzing, over and over, but he switches it to silent and ignores it. We leave the clerk's office and go to the attorneys. An hour after that, a dazed attorney has redrawn the deed and I sit with my pen poised over it, looking at Antoine. He gives me a slight nod, his eyes dark and serious.

I take a deep breath and look at the emerald gleaming on my hand. Then, for the third time that day, I sign my name: Harper Marigny.

Perhaps it is only that I know what that signature means. Perhaps it is no more than a reaction to the events of the day. But the moment my pen leaves the page, I feel a strange thud inside, as if something has shifted. I look up, startled, and see a faint frown creasing Antoine's brow, as if he has felt it too. A moment later, his phone rings again. He glances at it, and his frown deepens. He murmurs an apology, then takes the phone out of the room. I finish up with the attorney and walk outside to find him hanging up the phone. He faces me with a stark expression.

"We were too late." He takes my elbow and steers me toward the car.

"What do you mean, too late?" He opens the door and waits until I'm seated, then is around and in the other side with the uncanny speed he usually hides in public. The car purrs into life and he pulls out.

"Jeremiah got a call from Connor's phone an hour ago, while we were still in the clerk's office. He answered it but couldn't hear anything on the other end, just vague sounds, breathing. He waited but the line stayed open. He got worried, so he drove out to your place." I feel dread steal through my body in a cold shadow, sucking the sunlight from the day. "Your brother had opened the secret passage in the library. Jeremiah went down there." Antoine looks at me, his face grim. "The door to the cellar was open. He found Connor and Avery lying on the ground, unconscious."

"That's impossible." I swivel to face him, my mind refusing to process what he's saying. "Connor couldn't have opened that door. He said as much. He doesn't have the tools."

"Jeremiah was certain." Antoine is speeding down the road toward our house, taking each bend so fast it would normally terrify me. Today all I want is for him to go faster. "There's more." He pulls the car into the oak tunnel of our driveway. "The coffins that held Keziah and Caleb are open." He roars up the drive and comes to a halt in a cloud of dust. "We were too late, Harper. We changed the deed too late. They escaped the cellar while it was still in your maiden name—and now they're gone."

CHAPTER 20

FREED

*C*onnor's truck is parked below the stairs, a jackhammer in the back of it. My heart skips a beat, until I see the rental tag is still holding the zip closed. So that wasn't how they escaped, then.

Jeremiah meets us below the porch, his face pale and strained. "I closed the cellar door in case they come back," Jeremiah says to Antoine by way of greeting. "And I brought Connor and Avery to the library." He looks between us. "Why are you together?" His brows draw together. "And why are you dressed like that?"

"You explain," I say to Antoine, taking the stairs in a couple of leaps and going into the house. "And what do you mean, you brought Connor and Avery into the library? Are they okay?"

"Harper." I glance back at where Antoine is standing just beyond the door. "You have to invite me in. Keziah and Caleb could be anywhere. That door can't hold them anymore."

I hesitate. Only a couple of days ago, I stood right where he is now and swore that I would never invite him in. Even now, the thought of allowing him access to our home feels dangerous, as if once done, nothing can ever be the same. The emerald on my hand gleams in the sunlight. *Nothing will ever be the same regardless.* Antoine is watching me, one tapping finger against the doorframe betraying his tension.

Then I think of Connor and Avery, and whatever fears I have are replaced by far worse ones.

"Come in."

Antoine is inside and past me in a rush of air, gone. I hurry after him through the house to the library at the back. Connor and Avery are lying side by side on the floor. Marks in the dust show where Jeremiah has dragged them into the room. Antoine is leaning over them, and as I enter, he says in a muffled tone, "Don't come any closer, Harper."

I have no intention of listening to him and keep coming. "Jeremiah!" Antoine's voice is rough, and then I feel Jeremiah's arms, surprisingly strong, containing me. "Take her outside."

"No!" I struggle angrily. "Let me go. What's wrong with Connor?" I can hear the fear in my voice making it shrill. "Let me *go!*"

"Connor and Avery will both be alright. But you can't be in here." I pull against Jeremiah hard enough that I maneuver around to see Connor, pale and lifeless, with a gaping wound on his neck that terrifies me. Antoine has his wrist held over Connor's face. He turns his own head quickly to the side, out of view, but not before I see the blood on his mouth and the hard, bronze gleam in his eyes. "What are you doing?" I whisper. Antoine doesn't look at me. "What have you done to him?"

"He's helping them, Harper," says Jeremiah behind me. "The wound on Connor's neck wasn't made by Antoine."

Antoine is still turned away from me. "Get her out of here," he says roughly.

"Are you feeding him your *blood?*" I'm so revolted I feel physically sick.

"It's alright, Harper." Jeremiah tries to pull me away. "His blood will heal them. Please, trust me."

"I'm not leaving my brother here." I wrench myself from Jeremiah's grasp. My voice is calmer now, colder. "You can do what you want, but I'm not leaving Connor."

Antoine is bending over Avery, still turned away from me. "Is that true?" I ask his back. "Will your blood heal them?"

He nods, but doesn't look at me. "It will take a while. They've both lost a lot of blood." He turns his head sideways, but still away from me, looking toward the staircase. "When I go down, leave the stairwell open. Keziah and Caleb can't come up into the daylight. You'll be safe here—until nightfall."

"If they can't come up into the daylight, then where are they?" I'm confused.

"In the slave tunnels." Antoine's voice is grim. "They know every tunnel beneath this property. But the exits they once knew are all blocked. They won't be able to escape. Eventually they'll have to come back to the cellar. If they do, we can trap them there again."

"Are you sure?" I don't want to ask him directly about my name on the deed in front of Jeremiah.

"The binding is back in place. I felt it." Antoine stands up. "If we can get Keziah and Caleb into the cellar, I think I know how to close the door again." He glances down at Avery. "When she wakes up, ask Avery exactly what happened when they opened that door." When he turns, he looks as he always does, but his suit jacket sleeve has a dark smear where he's wiped the blood from his face.

I shudder. His pupils dilate then retract. It's only when the hard-slate mask returns that I realize the man I married today has just disappeared and been replaced by a cold, remote stranger.

Antoine turns away. "No matter what happens," he says, talking to Jeremiah rather than me, "you are not to go down into that cellar. Keziah and Caleb will be starving. It's a miracle that they didn't kill Avery and Connor. Even the scent of blood will be enough to draw them from anywhere in those tunnels, and down in the cellar and tunnels beyond, you are prey. If they find you, they will kill you. You must understand this." He doesn't look at me as he speaks. When Jeremiah nods, Antoine turns toward the bookshelf and pushes the button to open it. I rush over and kneel beside Connor, staring in horror at the gaping wound on his neck. I can't imagine how anyone could survive such an horrific injury; half of his throat has been torn away. Avery, on the other hand, has a much smaller wound, though she looks just as pale and lifeless as Connor.

"What about you?" I hear Jeremiah say behind me. "You can't go down there, Antoine. They'll kill you."

"I'll be fine."

"No!" I turn back to see Jeremiah standing with his fists clenched, eyes bright with unshed tears. "Please," he says, his voice breaking on the word. "Antoine. Don't go down there."

"It's alright, Jeremiah." There is something gentle in Antoine's voice, a kindness that is so at odds with the detached stranger of a moment ago that I swing back to look at him, but all I see is a rush of black suit jacket as he turns into the staircase and is gone.

I look back at Jeremiah, taking in his hectic color, his heaving chest, and look of absolute devastation as he stares after Antoine. He turns slowly back to me, and the distress on his face darkens.

"This is your fault," he says in a low, angry voice. "He's going to die because of you. And if he does," he says, his eyes boring furiously into mine, "I will never forgive you."

CHAPTER 21

MONSTERS

*J*eremiah slumps to the floor, back against the wall, hands loosely over his knees, head down. "Your brother and Avery will be fine." His voice is flat and he doesn't look at me. "It takes a while to work, but they'll get better, trust me."

"How do you know?" I'm still shaken by his anger of a moment ago, but it's hard to think of anything other than Connor and Avery while they're lying on the floor. Apart from the rise and fall of their chests, they look as if they are dead.

"Because Antoine saved me." Jeremiah glances at me then away again. "The night my parents died."

"Is that why you're defending him—because he didn't kill you?" My heart aches in sympathy. "Jeremiah, I know Antoine seems like he's helping us right now. But don't forget what he's done—what he is." I shake my head, wondering if its Jeremiah or myself I'm speaking to. "He's a vampire, Jeremiah. He drinks blood to survive." It's the first time I've said it aloud, and as I do, the cold reality of it drips like acid off my tongue. "He killed your parents, Jeremiah. How can you forgive him for that?"

Jeremiah's face grows darker as I speak, and by the time I finish, he looks almost as mad as the stories say his ancestors became. "Antoine didn't kill them. The night they died, my parents were wasted, Harper. They had me in the car with them. They were so wrecked they drove off the highway and died instantly. I would have died too, if Antoine hadn't found me."

"I didn't know that." I try to hide my surprise, wondering why Antoine let me believe otherwise. I'm not sure how much to say to Jeremiah, or what I can ask him. "I'm glad he saved you. But there's a lot you don't know about Antoine Marigny, Jeremiah. A long time ago, he did terrible things. He killed people, tortured them. And saving you was not done out of kindness. He saved you because you are the last living Marigny. He needed you, Jeremiah, to keep himself safe."

Jeremiah is frowning at me. "You have it all wrong," he says, shaking his head. "Honestly, Harper—you don't know anything."

"Oh, really." Annoyed, I look at him. "Believe me, if you want more, I can give you more." He looks away and makes a dismissive noise, then scuffs the ground.

"It doesn't matter," he mutters.

"Wait a minute." My eyes narrow. "Did Antoine tell you not to talk to me about this?" His silence is confirmation enough. "What is it I don't know? Jeremiah, tell me."

He meets my eyes resentfully. "If I tell you, will you let him stay?"

I'm taken aback. "Why would you want him to stay?"

"You came to our house this morning." His voice is not quite steady. "Do you think I always lived in a house like that, Harper? A proper home, with a fridge that was stocked, and a kitchen that was used for cooking something other than drugs?" I raise my eyebrows, but he carries on before I say anything. "Because I didn't. I was raised in a trailer so far on the wrong side of town people barely knew it existed unless they came looking for meth. The only thing my parents cared about was the next pipe they smoked. They didn't care about the family or doing their duty to Antoine."

"What duty?" I ask, confused.

"I'm a Marigny, Harper." He throws the words like stones. "We're taught the story of our family from the cradle. And I'm not the last living Marigny. There are others, overseas mostly. I was trying to track them down before my parents died, to ask them to take ownership of the mansion." He looks at me. "Our story is written down in the back of an old family bible. I can show you one day, if you like. Every generation of owners is told the story when they're children, then reminded of it, over and over. We have to sign the bible when we come of age, saying we understand what we've read, and that we will abide by our promise to keep the secret safe, the magic bound. My father signed that book," he says bitterly. "He knew what would happen if he sold the house. But he did it anyway, even knowing that it meant unleashing hell. He sold the mansion for nothing more than booze and meth. I didn't even know, until my parents picked me up from school in a new car with all our belongings and told me we were leaving town. They'd been drinking all day, buying rounds for everyone in town celebrating their big payout. That's when I called the number we had for Antoine and asked him to come back."

"You *asked* him to come back?"

Jeremiah nods. "He was already on his way. He told me later he felt it when the binding was broken." I remember earlier that day, when I signed my name on the deed, the odd shift in the air, like an invisible thud. *Yes, he would have felt it.*

"Regardless," I say, "none of that changes what he did. If you've read the story, then you know what he was, what the whole family was. You know he tortured slaves and made a deal to save his own family, then betrayed it."

"I think it's you who doesn't get what he did." Jeremiah meets my eyes steadily. "Antoine walked away from his family when he was barely older than we are now. He hated his father and brothers, even before Keziah and Caleb came and turned them from the evil they already were into the monsters you're talking about. Antoine had gone inland, working with Native American trappers. He'd bought a boat, started a trading company that had nothing to do with cotton, or slaves, or his family at all."

I stare at him in disbelief. "Then why is it his name on the treaty?"

"Keziah and Caleb couldn't walk in the daylight without help,"

Jeremiah said. "It was one of the slaves, Samuel, who recognized the symbol on the talismans they wore as being the magic that protected them. Without their talismans, they would burn in sunlight—even if they rose again from the ashes, as they had after previous attempts to kill them. If they could steal the talismans, Samuel said, then Keziah and Caleb could be captured in the house and he could bind them there—but to trap them, he would have to create a monster just as strong. To do that, he'd need blood from the Marigny family, since they owned the land. Atsila, the wife of the Natchez chief, the Great Sun, had powerful magic. She could work with the monster Samuel created, she said, empower it to walk in the sun. The Natchez knew Antoine. They had traded with him, knew what kind of man he was. They asked if he would give his blood to help bind the magic—if he would become their monster."

I'm hardly aware of the room anymore, or even of Connor and Avery's still forms lying beside me. Every word Jeremiah says seems to crack me open, forcing light and dark to intermingle. A line I had thought clear in my mind, between the *good* on one side and the *bad* on the other, is blurred and indistinct.

"Antoine refused. He hated his family and everything they stood for." Jeremiah's face darkens. "The plantation was in ruins, the fields around it burning for miles. Keziah and Caleb had captured Antoine's family. They fed them blood, too much of it. Their blood can heal—but too much, and it works like a drug, making the drinker impossibly strong and fast. And savage," he adds, glancing at me. "All Antoine's father and brothers wanted to do was to kill and destroy. The blood also made them sensitive to light. Nights at the mansion became hellish, violent. Antoine's father and brothers would bring female slaves inside the house and . . . toy with them." He clears his throat uncomfortably, his face red, before continuing. "Keziah and Caleb drank from the slaves as much as they wanted; there were always more slaves to buy. Still, Antoine would have walked away. He despised his father and brothers. But the Natchez, who were desperate, had taken his sister captive. They said they needed more than just Marigny blood—to be sure it would work, they had to bind the magic inside the actual body of a Marigny. Antoine was given a choice."

"His sister or him," I whisper. "They blackmailed him."

Jeremiah nodded. "Antoine was furious. But he did it. As the eldest son, the mansion would automatically fall to him on his father's death, so it also made the magic more powerful. He made a will bequeathing the mansion to his sister on his death. Then he pretended to return to the family and befriended Keziah and Caleb, along with his father and brothers. For days, weeks, he played their sadistic games—the Natchez told him he could only become a vampire after he drank Keziah's blood, and it took time before she trusted him to give it. His father and brothers didn't know how vampires were made. Keziah and Caleb kept it secret, baiting them with the promise of immortality. But Samuel knew, and he told the Natchez. They waited until Antoine had drunk, not once, but several times, until Keziah trusted him. The final time he drank, he took more than usual, and when Keziah's back was turned, he spat it into a jar and sealed it. That night, after Keziah and Caleb went back to their cellar just before the dawn, Antoine took a knife to his own father, killing him and automatically transferring ownership of the mansion into his own name. Then he turned the knife on himself." Jeremiah meets my eyes soberly. "Antoine had to allow his body to be completely drained of blood, almost to the point of death. The Natchez watched over him as he did, then fed him Keziah's blood that he had saved. None of them knew for sure if it would work or not. He could have died, then and there."

I gasp, my hand coming up involuntarily to cover my mouth. I can't imagine the strength it would have taken to do that to himself, knowing that he would either die forever—or be reborn as a monster.

"The Natchez kept him safe throughout the day and night it took for him to transition, hiding both his father's body and Antoine from Keziah and Caleb. Then, in the final moments before Antoine changed form, at first light of dawn, Atsila, the wife of the Natchez chief, worked her sun magic into Antoine's body."

"The totem," I say. "The one tattooed at the base of his spine."

"Yes. That day, he became immortal—by feeding on the Natchez woman who worked the magic, Atsila herself, draining her to death. That was the Natchez sacrifice to the magic: the life of the greatest of their own."

"Why?" I can't imagine why anyone would offer themselves in such a way. "Why would the Natchez make such a sacrifice?"

"The Natchez had suffered too, don't forget. And alone they didn't have the power to hold Keziah and Caleb. I guess they wanted to ensure the safety of their people—not that it helped, in the end." Jeremiah shakes his head, frowning. "There's some story about Antoine's sister and a Natchez man, but when I asked, Antoine wouldn't talk about it, and my parents didn't know so much. All I know for sure is that the Natchez kept her safe, until it was over.

"Caleb and Keziah didn't know he'd transitioned," Jeremiah continues. "He walked in the daylight like normal, without a talisman of any kind. They had no reason to suspect him. He took them by surprise and stole their talismans, then got them to the cellar and held them there. Newly made, vampires are stronger, for a while at least, than others. Antoine knew that if the binding was gonna work, he would have to stay in the cellar, holding them, until it was completed." Jeremiah looks at me grimly, his face oddly reminiscent of Antoine's in the same mood. "He went into that cellar knowing he'd be stuck there forever, desiccating next to the monsters that destroyed his family."

"How?" I whisper. "How did he escape?"

"His brothers." Jeremiah nods at the staircase. "The cellar was sealed closed by the Natchez with their totem on both sides, locking the magic inside. They blocked the tunnels, too, in case anything happened to break the binding on the cellar. But Antoine's brothers were furious. Their father was dead, and their sister had a will stating she got to inherit the plantation. They had been cheated, as they saw it, of both their property and their chance at immortality. Even without drinking more of the vampires' blood, they were plenty cruel. They tracked down the medicine man who'd done the binding spell and tortured him for days, until finally they made him agree to break it. The brothers dug a hole through to the cellar from the field and waited for night to break the cellar door open.

"Antoine could hear them coming. He knew what would happen if their plan succeeded. Knowing Caleb and Keziah couldn't leave during the day, he broke the seal himself before night fell. It had been weeks since he had fed. He was half mad with thirst when he got out, and he tore his own brothers to pieces. The Natchez and the medicine man closed the seal again before nightfall, trapping Keziah and Caleb, but this time with Antoine on the other side. But breaking the binding had consequences."

"Keziah found a way through," I whisper, barely able to imagine even half the story I've just heard. "She found a way to reach the minds of others."

"Yes. Antoine isn't a monster, Harper. He was forced to become what he is. And even if he did it reluctantly, he still did it, and lost everything in the process. He killed his own father and his brothers to save his sister, and stop an evil that he knew might otherwise never be stopped. That's why every Marigny who inherits this mansion is taught their duty. Antoine paid a greater price than anyone should ever have to. He carries this weight, this immortal curse, to watch over the binding and ensure that those creatures never escape again." His face crumbles. "My parents failed in that duty. It's our fault that he had to come back here. All of this is my fault."

CHAPTER 22

TOTEM

"No." I reach for Jeremiah's hand, my heart breaking at the grief and anger in his voice. "This isn't your fault, Jeremiah." But he turns away from me, anger and shame reddening his face.

On the floor, Avery is stirring. She moans and then opens her eyes, staring up at me.

"Harper?" she murmurs weakly.

"Avery?" I lean over her, holding her up so I can give her a drink of water. "Don't try to get up. You're still weak." Then I give Jeremiah a questioning look. "That's right, isn't it? She's still weak?" I have no idea how vampire blood works as a cure. He nods.

"It will take a few hours before she's back to normal."

"Harper." Avery clutches my hand, her beautiful, almond-shaped eyes wide and anxious. "We need to leave! There's something in the cellar, something bad. It attacked Connor—" she glances sideways and sees Connor lying next to her. "Connor!" She rolls to her side, touching the blood at his neck, her face horrified. In the time Jeremiah and I have been talking, though, his wound has completely healed, and her hand comes away dry. Relief courses through me with such intensity I'm almost lightheaded. I touch Connor hesitantly, needing to feel his pulse for myself. For a moment I think I will actually faint for the first time in my life. I realize that somewhere between Jeremiah's phone call and this moment, I began looking into the abyss of a life without Connor. It felt so unbelievably lonely and cold that now I feel shaky and uncertain, as if my body has been reassembled in a new form.

I'm clearly not the only one who feels that way, though for different reasons. Looking confused, Avery touches her own neck, where her wound has also healed. "I thought—" she shakes her head, then smiles uncertainly. "I must have been really out of it. Where did all the blood come from?"

I remember what Antoine said before he left, about asking for her story. "Avery." I try to sound reassuring, while still deflecting her question. "What do you remember about what happened to you?"

"I came to see Connor. I'd baked some cookies." I nod encouragingly. She looks at me and flushes. "They were kind of special cookies," she mumbles.

"Special?"

Jeremiah rolls his eyes. "I thought you were from the city. Weed cookies, Harper."

"Oh. Right." I look at Connor. "And my brother ate them?" Connor's always hated drugs of any kind, mainly because his father is so fond of them.

"Not exactly." Her color deepens. "I maybe didn't tell him what was in them," she says, dropping her eyes.

"Okay." I don't even want to think about why she thought getting my brother high without his knowledge was a good idea, but there's no point dwelling on it now. "So what happened then?"

"It was really strong stuff. We got a little ripped. Then I started hearing voices." She looks shamefaced. "Well, at least, it seemed that way." I want to tell her that I know exactly what she means, but I figure that's probably not wise, so I let it go. "Anyhow, Connor was kind of chilled out, so I went for a walk through the house. I was just so sure I could hear someone calling me, you know? It was weird. Then Connor must have woken up, because all of a sudden, he was in the library with me. He said he wanted to show me something cool.

He pressed a button or something and that bookshelf thing opened. Connor said we shouldn't go down the stairs, but I was pretty far gone, so I just went anyway. He was behind me, laughing and telling me to come back up, but then I tripped and cut my hand." She turns her hand palm upward and frowns. "Well, I thought I did," she says uncertainly.

"You were out of it, Avery. You probably imagined it." I can't look at Jeremiah.

"Maybe." She still looks unconvinced. "It was so weird, it's like a dream now. I can hardly remember anything except the door at the bottom of the stairs. It was big and heavy and had some sort of symbol in the middle of it." She shakes her head. "All I could think about was touching that symbol. It's like it was calling to me." She looks at me apologetically. "I was really out of it."

"That doesn't matter." I try not to sound impatient. "Do you remember what happened next?"

"Well, I did touch it. And then something happened. I don't know what it was. I think I must have been hallucinating or something. It was like the symbol started moving, and glowing, and then the door started to swing open. Connor was yelling behind me and something inside the cellar moved—and that's it." She shakes her head. "That's all I remember. The next thing I know, I was waking up here on the floor, with you bending over me." She looks at me as if she's seeing me properly for the first time. "Why are you dressed like that? And why weren't you at school today?"

Jeremiah and I exchange a look. "It was my fault," he says, smiling at her. "Harper had to come to the attorney's office with Antoine and I to sign some papers about the house. I drove Harper home and we found this bookcase thing open. When I went down the stairs, I found you and Connor under some old timbers. They must have knocked you out. I had to pull them off you and drag you upstairs. Got a bit bloody in the process, I guess. I'm sorry about that."

Avery looks at Connor's blood-spattered body, and her own, also liberally sprayed. "Oh," she says uncertainly. "Wow. I must have been really out of it."

"Why don't you go upstairs to my room?" I imagine her going back to her parents covered in blood and wince. "You can wash up in the bathroom. There are fresh T-shirts on the hanging rack. Probably best if you leave that one here for me to wash."

"What about Connor?" She looks at him anxiously. "Shouldn't he be in the hospital or something?"

"He's fine. He woke up a little while ago," I lie. "He just needs some rest."

"He's going to be so mad with me."

"He probably won't remember any of it." I smile, avoiding Jeremiah's eyes. This is one time I will definitely support the use of compulsion. The last thing I need is for Avery's stoned brain to recover her memories.

I wait until she's gone then turn to Jeremiah. "We need to get her out of here. Can you drive her home?"

He shakes his head. "It's better if you take her. You'll both be safer."

"I'm not leaving Connor." I glance at the window. The shadows are growing, but dusk is a ways off. "And there's still enough time to go and come back before it gets dark." He looks unsure, but then Avery comes back downstairs, chewing her lip. She's washed up and changed clothes, at least, I'm relieved to see. "Maybe I should just go back downstairs. I must still be wasted. I would swear I could hear that voice again."

Jeremiah jumps to his feet. "Come on." He forces a smile. "I'll drive you home in your car."

Avery looks at me apologetically. "I'm so sorry about all this, Harper." She laughs shakily. "My love life really is a disaster area."

"Don't worry about it. Just let Jeremiah drive you home, and get some rest. I'll take care of Connor."

"Thanks." She casts a final, confused look at the open bookcase and yawning stairway beyond it and visibly shivers. "You should probably close that thing up. It's dangerous."

"Yes." I give her a little wave goodbye. "I'm starting to realize that."

CHAPTER 23

SEAL

*T*he house is silent with Jeremiah and Avery gone. Connor is still out. I guess the worse the injuries are, the longer it takes for the blood cure to work.

Everything Jeremiah told me swirls in the still, silent room amid the scent of magnolias and the light shimmering from the emerald on my hand.

I thought I'd married a monster. Somehow, that bargain is easier for me to reconcile than marriage to the man Jeremiah described. What am I supposed to do about that man? How am I supposed to discard him? Asking Antoine to leave would deprive Jeremiah of the family he clearly craves.

I don't want to think about the other reasons I don't want him to leave. Those are too complicated to even begin to imagine. I think of the way he kissed me in the church, the way he looked at me when I asked him if he would wear his wedding ring.

Always.

I shiver as I imagine what *always* might mean to a vampire who has already lived for centuries.

My phone vibrates and seeing Antoine's number, I snatch it up.

"Harper." The line is bad, and his voice is indistinct. "They got away. You need to—" the rest of his words are lost in static.

"Antoine." I check the reception but mine is fine. "Are you still underground? I can't hear you."

"When Avery wakes up . . ."

"Antoine!" The line crackles again and drops out. I stare at the blank screen and a moment later a text comes through: *They are coming. Tell Avery to seal door before dark.* I text back: *How?* and stare at the phone, waiting for an answer. And waiting.

Nothing comes. I think of calling Jeremiah and asking him to bring Avery back. But she didn't understand how she opened the door anyway, and remembering her face, dazed and upset, I can't imagine how I would begin to explain what I need her to do, or why. I think back to the truce that was signed. I think of Cass's mom telling me about the curse: *So long as a living Marigny owns it, and Natchez blood seals it . . .*

Avery is Natchez, I think. That must be why she could open the door. But is it only a Natchez person that unlocks the door—or is it Natchez blood?

I hear a noise from downstairs and stiffen, listening. It comes again, the unmistakeable sound of movement. Then a voice: *Help me . . .*

Cold fear clutches my throat. I glance at Connor, still unconscious. Outside the day lingers, but the sky has changed to the burnished golds of dusk. Night will soon fall. And once it does, Keziah and Caleb will be free to come upstairs, into the house. To take anyone they choose.

Help me. I think of Avery saying that she heard the voice. I pull out my phone and press the recording app. "Who's there?" I call, watching the line on the voice app make jagged spikes in response.

"Help me." The line on the app spikes. The voice is no longer in my mind. Keziah is speaking to me.

The thought stills my blood to a slow, thick pulse that almost hurts in my veins. "Keziah? Is that you?"

"We need your help." Her voice is soft and seductive, caressing. I

LUCY HOLDEN

stare blankly at the wall, willing my brain to work, to think of something.

"What do you need me to do?" I ask. "I've read the history, Keziah. I know you're trapped against your will. Tell me how to help you." I'm trying to stall her, to buy myself time to help.

"Come down," she says. "Come down so I can see you." Keziah's voice is clearer than before. I hear her as if she is inside me, her words seeming to exist alongside my own thoughts, like two branches of a river divided by a strip of land. I don't think she can hear my thoughts, not unless I'm speaking to her. I hope not.

"I'm afraid." I take my heels off as I speak. Glancing at Connor, I creep from the room and up the stairs, praying that Avery was too dazed to collect all her clothes. "I don't understand how you can speak to me."

"You are upstairs," her voice says in my mind. "Why? We are down here."

I almost sigh with relief when I see Avery's blood-covered T-shirt on the floor. I pick it up and creep back down the stairs to the library.

"I told you." I pause at Connor's side. "I'm afraid."

I open my text messaging app. *Shut cellar from tunnel*, I text to Antoine's phone. I pray he gets it.

"Don't be afraid." Her voice is soft again. "Free us, and you will live a life you could only dream of. An immortal life."

"How do I free you?" I move toward the stairs. "What must I do?"

"The tunnels are blocked." Her voice changes, becomes sharper. "And we have an enemy who roams them, seeking us."

Antoine. I think it, then extend the thought out and allow her to hear it.

"He betrayed us." Keziah's voice hisses angrily. "Now he seeks to kill us. You must unblock one of the tunnels."

She definitely can't hear me unless I answer her. I remember Antoine saying he'd tried to compel me, the day on the dock. Maybe it's the same for Keziah—she can talk to me, but not control me.

"I can't do that," I say. "It would take weeks—months. Come up the

128

stairs. There is nobody here who will hurt you." I try to sound excited. "I've seen your face in my dreams. I've drawn it."

"We cannot enter the cellar." I can hear the tension in her voice.

"Why not?" I ask. There is a short pause, and I hear the soft sibilance of whispers. I smile grimly.

"We're afraid of it." Keziah makes her voice timid. "We have been trapped in it a long time."

"The door is open." I realize I'm mimicking the old-fashioned cadence of her speech. "You need only pass through the cellar to come upstairs." I glance at the window. "Night is falling. There is nothing to harm you."

"We do not trust easily. You will give me your blood," she says in a low voice. Her words hold a note of command that reminds of me of Antoine speaking to the priest. She is trying to compel me. I can feel it. "Let us drink of you until you die. Then we will be free."

I think of the priest at the church repeating Antoine's words and take a deep breath. "I will give you my blood," I say, striving for an even tone. "I will let you drink of me until I die. Then you will be free."

"Good." I hear the triumphant note in her voice and tense, clutching the T-shirt in my hand. "Now," Keziah says, "come down the stairs so I can see you."

My hands shake as I wrap the shirt around one of them, making sure the most blood-soaked material is splayed over my palm. I have no idea if my hunch is right. If I'm wrong, these steps will likely be my last. I don't have time to think about it, and part of me knows that if I do, I'll never find the strength to continue. Instead I put one foot in front of another, trying not to imagine anything beyond the next step.

As I descend, the charred stench grows more rancid, the air colder. I step over the landing and the cellar yawns before me, so dark it takes a moment for my eyes to adjust. Then I see a flicker of white at the far end.

"Keziah." I come slowly down the stairs. "My name is Harper. I will help you."

"Yes. I have felt you before now." The flicker of white is a rotted strip of blouse that breaks the darkness as she moves from the tunnel into the cellar. "Come closer, Harper. Remember your promise." Her tone is low and compelling.

"I will come closer," I repeat mechanically. "I remember my promise." As my eyes adjust to the gloom, I can see only one figure. I tense. If Caleb is still in the tunnel, Antoine is in danger. I'm still descending the stairs, keeping my face neutral and my eyes unfocused, but I'm starting to worry. Keziah turns to me and I see her face for the first time, just as I drew it. She glances behind her again. I have three steps to go. "Come, Caleb," she says commandingly.

I see the second shadow slip into the room, then stillness explodes into action.

"Now!" It's Antoine's voice, and Keziah swings around, snarling with fury. In the same movement, she lunges for the door on my side just as I push it closed, hurling myself at it with the bloodstained shirt held up against the embossed totem on the door. It slams closed just as her body lands heavily against it. I feel a hard, superhuman strength shake the door and know I can't hold out against it, but then the totem begins to glow and writhe on the iron. The door sucks inward with a hard finality, binding itself against me and melding to the wall, locking the cellar closed once again.

"Antoine!" I call, but I can hear nothing from within the cellar. It's as if all sound has been sucked behind the seal. The last of the iron clicks into place, the glow fades, and the cellar is still and silent, as if Keziah has never been.

CHAPTER 24

TUNNELS

I race upstairs, sick with dread and tension. Connor is half-propped up on the floor, rubbing a hand over his face. "Harper." He shakes his head in bemusement. "I don't know what happened." He looks down at his shirt. "Why am I covered in blood?"

"Avery fed you weed cookies and got you stoned. You fell down the stairs." I crouch beside him. "Connor. That jackhammer you rented. Do you think you can use it?"

"The jackhammer?" He looks at me in confusion. "What's going on?" He glances around. "Where's Avery?"

"Avery's fine. Jeremiah took her home. Connor, I know this is confusing, but someone is in trouble, and I need your help. I don't have time to explain everything, but I will, I promise." I wince internally, knowing this, at least, is a lie. I can't imagine a day when I will be remotely able to explain any of this to my brother. I push my misgivings aside. "Can you use the jackhammer or not?"

He looks out the window. "At night?" Then, seeing my face, "Yes, Harper. I can use it."

"Good." I pull him to his feet.

He looks me up and down. "Why are you dressed like that?"

I go through to the kitchen and reach for the old boots leaning up against the doorway. "I'm getting tired," I mutter as I pull them on, "of people asking me that question." I grab the hurricane lamp as headlights turn up the drive, and Jeremiah tumbles out of Avery's car carrying a duffle bag. "They're in the cellar," I say briefly as he runs over. "But Antoine is still in the tunnels."

"Antoine?" Connor's brows lower. "What's going on, Harper?"

"Remember that concrete cover you showed me, to the side of the house? We need to break through that so I can get into the tunnels that lead to the hurricane cellar. Now." I meet my brother's eyes. "Do you trust me, Connor?"

He searches my face, then nods. "Of course I do."

"Then please," I say. "Help us."

The truck bounces over the uneven ground. Connor parks so the headlights beam on the concrete, and we unload the jackhammer from the back. Jeremiah eyes it uneasily. "Have you ever actually used one of these before?" he asks Connor.

Connor shrugs. "I've seen one used."

Jeremiah laughs hollowly. "Reassuring."

I lean down, putting my ear against the concrete. "Antoine!" I call. "We've got a jackhammer. We're going to get you out."

Jeremiah takes my arm and pulls me up. "Harper," he says in a low voice. "What if more comes out of that tunnel than Antoine?"

"I sealed the door from my side. And I think Antoine sealed it from his. But if not, he's trapped down there with them. Either way, he can't stay there, Jeremiah." He looks at me, then the concrete.

"Well, we better get ready for whatever comes out of there." He pulls the duffel bag out of the back of the truck and opens it, revealing a bundle of wooden stakes.

I shake my head. "Those won't kill them."

"They'll slow them down," says Jeremiah grimly.

Connor is pulling on gloves. He looks at the bag, then at me as if he's never seen me before. "Please, Connor," I lie. "I promise I'll explain when this is done." He shakes his head and pointedly puts earplugs in. He hauls the jackhammer to the concrete covering the entrance to the tunnels and turns it on. The noise is deafening.

Connor lowers his face shield and drills down. Jeremiah and I stand back, each holding a stake. It seems to take forever, headlights catching the concrete dust in the air. Connor holds it steady, every muscle straining. He pauses at one point and looks at my face, then shakes his head and starts again. Gradually the drill cuts down, through concrete and rock, until a darker layer is revealed. Connor turns off the hammer. Stepping back, he raises his mask. "I can't widen it without different tools." He eyes me. "What happens when I cut through, Harper?"

"Please." I stare at the concrete. "Antoine is down there, Connor."

"Maybe that's the best place for him." His eyes shift to Jeremiah then back to me. "I didn't really fall down any stairs, did I? What came out of that cellar, Harper?"

"Antoine isn't the same as what came out of the cellar." Jeremiah steps forward. "You have to cut through, Connor. If they've found Antoine, he could already be close to death."

"Get me in there." I stare at the hole in the ground. He's under there, alone somewhere in those tunnels. Or even worse, in the cellar. I shudder. I can't think about that.

Connor's mouth tightens. He stalks to the truck and takes a saw. "For what it's worth," he mutters as he passes me, "I think this is a bad idea."

"Just do it, Connor. Please." The look he gives me could do the cutting for him, but he kneels and gets to work anyway.

"Harper." Jeremiah pulls me aside. "Antoine would have heard us drilling from a mile away. If he were unharmed, he would have punched through."

"Then he's harmed." I shake his arm off. "And I'm going down there."

"No. I'll go."

"Jeremiah." I look at him. "You're the only living Marigny here."

He looks pointedly at the ring on my hand. I color. I take it that Jeremiah is now party to our secret. "You're too important," I say. "Antoine wouldn't want you down there, I know it. And even if you went, I'd still go. Please, let me do this."

He holds my eyes then pulls me in for a brief, hard hug. "Bring him back," he says hoarsely.

I nod. "I will."

Connor steps back. I crouch down and start to clear the rubble away. The hole is barely big enough for me to slip through. I lower my legs, bracing myself on the sides, but glancing down, the drop is too far. I hold out a hand to Connor. "Lower me down."

He grasps my hands and I slide down. The ground is barely a foot below. "Okay," I say. Connor doesn't release me. I look up. "Connor. Let me go."

He grips my hands so hard it hurts. "I can't lose you, Harper," he says roughly. "Please don't do this."

I know his fear. I felt it myself, only recently, when I thought he was dead. But to my surprise, the fear I feel for Antoine is no less visceral. I don't really understand it. I only know that from the moment I kissed him in that church, Antoine became part of me, just as Connor is. I can no sooner leave him down there to die as I could let Tessa go without trying, at least, to save her.

"I have to." I press his fingers and force a smile. "I can't leave him, Connor. I couldn't live with myself. Please." I stare at him until he looks away, resignation darkening his eyes. "Let me go, Connor." He shakes his head, his mouth hard, but he does as I ask. I fall to the ground.

The tunnel is dark and silent. The faint scent of charred, dead fire lingers in the air. "Antoine?" I wait while my eyes adjust to the light. "Where are you?" The air is silent. I can't hear anything. I turn toward the direction of the cellar and stumble along the narrow passage. It is utterly black. I bounce from the rock faces on either side, horribly aware that I'm making enough noise to alert any predator lurking in the darkness. I was so sure Antoine had closed the other door, but now I question what I saw. Surely if was in the tunnels, he would hear me calling him.

The charred stench grows stronger. I'm nearing the cellar. The air about me is silent as a tomb. I can feel the cellar coming closer, like a dark chill reaching for me, and dread pulls at my chest. My foot strikes something and I tumble. I hear a grunt of pain and bend down. "Antoine?" I whisper. "Is that you?"

"Harper." His hand curls around my face. "I thought I was dreaming. You shouldn't be here." His voice is hoarse with pain.

"We've drilled through the concrete. I'm getting you out of here." I lean down and pull his arm over my shoulder. "It's not far."

"No." He refuses to rise. "You need to leave me here."

"What?" I crouch in front of him trying to look into his eyes, but the blackness is so complete I can't see them.

"I should have died down here." His hand holds my face. "I meant to die down here, Harper. I never should have escaped."

"But you did." I find the hard plane of his jaw, warm and vital beneath my touch. "You were made with the sun inside you. You were never meant to die in the darkness, Antoine."

"How did you close the cellar?" His thumb strokes my cheekbone.

"Avery's T-shirt." I smile beneath his touch. "I put it over my hand. The blood was enough to close the seal."

"I was terrified when I saw you there."

"When you told me to close it, I realized what you meant." I can feel the rasp of his stubble beneath my hand. "Jeremiah told me you were made by drinking the blood of a Natchez woman. That means you can activate the seal, too."

"I wasn't sure." His hand covers mine. "I didn't know if that blood lived in me or was gone. And I didn't know if you would understand what I meant about Avery closing it."

"I wasn't sure either." I laugh shakily. "But it worked, Antoine. They're locked inside." I turn my face into his hand. "Why didn't you tell me the real story?" I whisper. "Why did you let me believe that all those terrible things I accused you of were true?"

"Because it doesn't matter. None of it changes what I am."

I shake my head in his hand. "Of course it matters. It changes everything."

"Harper." I can feel the edge of his mouth against my hand. "Those terrible stories might not have been true at the beginning. But every one of them has been true in the years since. I know what I am. You need to understand it, too." His lips curl against my hand, as if he's steeling himself to say something. "All the books and movies lie, Harper. We don't shine in the sun. We don't live off animals, or blood banks, or other vampires. We might not need to kill, but we do need human blood to survive."

"We can talk about this later. We need to get out of here."

"No." His voice is faint. His head lolls against my hand, and his own falls away from my face. "You," he whispers. "You can go."

"We're going together."

"Harper." He is barely whispering. "She bit me. Keziah. She all but drained me." His jaw tenses under my touch. "I'm blood-starved," he breathes. "You're not safe with me. I'm good as dead—and you need to leave."

"You're a vampire. You can't die."

I feel him smile beneath my hand. "I can fade, Harper. Become dormant. Leave me here. I can be what I was intended to be at the first —their guard and keeper. I can keep you safe."

"So you're just going to give up?" I stand up. "After almost three centuries, Antoine, this is how you die?"

"It's my choice, Harper."

Anger churns inside me like a sickness. "My mother died of cancer, Antoine. My sister died because she got a stupid infection. My father died before I ever even knew him. But you are just going to lie down in a tunnel and die, not because you can't live, but because you can't be *bothered* to live." The words are bitter in my mouth. "If you drink blood, Antoine, you can't 'fade,' as you put it, right? So what if I do this?" I scrape my arm across a jagged point on the tunnel and the salty, metallic smell of blood fills the still air. I start to walk away. "And this?" I scrape the other one, leaving a trail of blood in my wake. "What will you do now, Antoine?"

"Harper." He rasps my name. "If I touch you, I'll drain you. Don't you understand? I'm starving."

"We swore before God, Antoine. Until death do us part."

"But death already has." He's right behind me, so close I can feel the heat of his breath. "I've been dead a long time, Harper. Let me go."

I turn around and hold up my arm, exposing the open cut. "No."

"Walk away, Harper." His voice is deepening, losing control.

"Drink." I step closer, feel the heat of him against me.

"I can't." I hear the last husk of restraint in his voice. "I'll kill you."

"No. You won't, Antoine. I know you won't." I take the last step forward and hear him inhale sharply, feel him poised above me, his hand barely skimming my throat, as if he hardly dares touch it, my skin tingling with an odd tension.

"Do it," I say.

CHAPTER 25

COMPULSION

One hand cradles the back of my head and the other is at the base of my spine. He draws me against him as his teeth sink into my neck, and I gasp at the shock. Then it is all sensation: my head falling into his hand, his palm splayed over my lower back, our bodies locked in a slow, sensual dance as all that I am flows into him. I can feel it, not painful as I thought it would be, but something deeper and more elemental, the essence of me drawn into his body and something of his flowing into mine. I start to fall into it, a warm, welcoming darkness that I want to be lost in. Then he pulls free, his head back, gasping with the effort of breaking the connection, and he spins me around as he sinks his own teeth into his wrist and holds it to my mouth. "Drink," he says hoarsely, and I am still caught in the magic of it and do as he commands, feeling the heat of him hit my body in an exotic, intoxicating rush. It isn't blood as I know it, but something thick and sweet, darkly seductive.

He curls me into him, his hand around my face, my back to his chest, stroking my hair. I hear him gasp as I drink him in. "Enough," he says in a low voice after a few moments, taking it away from my mouth. "Too much is bad." I swing around, his blood surging through my veins, sealing the cuts on my arm and neck, racing into every cell, making my skin tingle and senses reel. I reach up and he meets my mouth with his own, groaning as he takes it. His hand is entangled in my hair and he tugs at the pin holding it, so it falls down against the silk dress. He crushes me against him, holding me as he did when he drank from me, his large hand warm through the thin material. I'm so lost in sensation I press closer, arching against him so he makes a rough sound in his throat and lifts me against the wall, hitching my leg up and cupping the curve of my backside, his other hand entwined with mine on the cold stone above.

I hear someone calling my name, gradually becoming more insistent. I ignore it until Antoine pulls away from me. I make a noise of protest.

"Harper!" Connor's voice echoes from a distance, sharp with anxiety. "Where are you? Are you alright?"

"You need to answer him," says Antoine hoarsely against my neck.

"I'm fine, Connor," I gasp.

"You don't sound fine. I'm coming down there."

Antoine puts his head back, his body still hard against my own. "We need to leave," he says, his voice rough.

"I know," I whisper. I swallow hard. "Connor!" I call out. "I'm okay, truly. Don't come down here. We're on our way." We walk slowly through the tunnel, Antoine's hands on my hips from behind, his lips skimming the nape of my neck as we go. "You do realize," he murmurs, "that technically, this is our wedding night?"

The hole in the tunnel roof comes into view and I halt just beyond reach of prying eyes. "What happens," I whisper, "when we leave this tunnel?"

Behind me, he gathers my hair in one large hand and twists it, so it tumbles forward over my shoulder, his arms sliding around my waist and pulling me back against him. "What do you want to happen?" he murmurs against my ear.

"Harper!" Connor leans down into the tunnel, and I leap away from Antoine as if I've been electrocuted, suddenly aware of how disheveled I must look, my hair a wild mess, a bloodstained dress dirty and torn in places. I glance back at Antoine. "Do I have blood on my face?"

He shakes his head. The pale light streaming from the open sky above shows him in crumpled dress shirt, sleeves rolled up, hands thrust into his pockets and eyes gleaming with a heat that makes my blood race all over again. "Don't look at me like that," I mutter, turning away from him. I hear his low laugh and feel color heat my cheeks. I will never be able to face Connor like this.

I take a deep breath and step into Connor's range of sight. "See?" I say, my voice still slightly unsteady. "Fine, like I said."

Connor looks behind me to Antoine, and his face darkens. "Help her up," he orders.

Antoine nods, though his mouth is half-curled in amusement. "Your brother does not approve," he murmurs as he leans down to lift me up. I try to ignore the fact that his arms are right beneath my butt, and his face is buried against my belly, a situation I swear he takes full advantage of as Connor's hands grasp mine. Antoine's hands trail lazily down my body as Connor pulls me out of the tunnel, leaving a fiery line right to the ends of my feet and my breath coming short by the time I am out and standing on the cool grass. Connor turns back to the hole as if debating whether or not to go back. Antoine solves the issue by simply leaping up and pulling himself through, landing easily on the ground beside Connor, his eyes glittering with amusement at Connor's visible shock. "I think it's a little late for pretense," he says calmly. "Wouldn't you agree?"

Connor stares at him with open hostility. "I think you've got a lot of explaining to do. None of which I want to hear right now."

Antoine inclines his head politely, but the faint smile lurking at the corners of his mouth does nothing to lessen Connor's scowl. My brother turns to me. "You're coming back to the house with me." He frowns and turns back to Antoine. "That is," he says, "assuming it is safe for us to go inside?"

Antoine's smile fades and his eyes narrow faintly and swivel to me, as if trying to ascertain how much he can say. "It is," I say hastily, then wonder what on earth I'm going to tell my brother.

"But whatever is under there," Connor says, staring down at the tunnel opening, "it isn't going to stay locked up forever, is it?" I open my mouth to answer, then see the growing frown on Antoine's face and close it again. What am I going to tell Connor? That Keziah and Caleb will never threaten us again? No matter what happened today, regardless of how well the seal on the cellar door worked, part of me knows deep down that this isn't done. I can feel Antoine studying me as I weigh my answer.

"We've done everything we can to ensure they can't escape," I say quietly.

"They," Connor repeats flatly. "There's more than one—thing—down there?" When I don't answer, his mouth tightens into a grim line. He looks between Antoine and me. "And by we, I take it you mean him."

"Connor." I start to speak, but he pushes past me and addresses Antoine instead. "I don't know what you are," he says slowly, "but whatever it is, my sister doesn't need it in her life, and neither do I." He stares at Antoine long enough to make his meaning utterly clear, then turns to me. "We're leaving," he says shortly. "We're not staying another night in that house."

I wince. Antoine is standing behind Connor with his arms folded, watching me with raised eyebrows, asking a silent question. I know what I should do. But Connor is my brother, the only family I have left. The thought of lying to him doesn't just hurt. It tears me apart.

"No," I say, catching his arm. "Please, Connor. I've taken care of it. I've made sure you can still restore the mansion, do everything you dreamed of. We're going to be fine."

"Taken care of it?" Connor gestures impatiently, taking in my ragged appearance, the blood on my dress. "Harper, you look like you've been in a war zone. The last thing I remember is seeing some monster sink its teeth into Avery's neck. I woke up on the floor, covered in blood and feeling like I've been pumped full of the most powerful drug never invented, to then use a jackhammer to blast open a tunnel that only days ago you made me swear I wouldn't touch." He seizes my hand and holds it up. The moonlight catches the emerald, making it gleam with green fire. "Now you're wearing a ring on your wedding finger which, I happen to know, since I've researched every aspect of this house, is the long-lost Marigny emerald, worth more than the damned mansion itself and not so much as glimpsed for over two hundred years." He looks at me grimly. "Are you still going to tell me that you've 'taken care' of things, Harper? Because it looks to me like you're so far out of your depth you're close to drowning."

Every word strikes home with the painful clarity of truth, driving shards of ice into the heat that only moments ago coursed through my veins. I know he's right. I know things have gotten out of control. We came here for a better life, a new start, and instead I've found us death, destruction, and a houseful of monsters, one of whom I'm actually married to.

I take a deep breath and look at Antoine. "Do it," I say quietly.

"Are you sure?" Antoine looks intently at me, ignoring Connor's scowling face. I nod. I can feel tears welling up and I can't look at Connor. "You don't have to watch this," Antoine says.

"Watch what?" Connor's eyes are darkening. He starts toward Antoine with murder in his eyes.

"Do it," I whisper, and Antoine takes Connor's shoulders.

"Be calm and listen."

Connor stills immediately. His eyes glaze over, become unfocused.

Jeremiah takes my arm gently. "He's right, Harper," he says quietly. "You don't have to watch this."

"Yes, I do," I whisper, staring at my brother. "I have to watch it all."

Antoine's face is dark and set. "You and Avery got high, had fun," he says to Connor. "You showed her the secret staircase, and it partly collapsed on you both. You feel a little foolish now, because you know there's nothing interesting in the cellar and that the stairs are dangerous, so after today you are going to board up the staircase and never open the bookcase, go near it, or mention it to anyone, ever again. Jeremiah and I accidentally made a hole in the tunnel, but we'll fix it tonight, and you won't have to touch it or worry about it. You'll never think about cutting into any of the tunnels again." He glances over Connor's shoulder at me. As his eyes travel slowly over my torn dress and bloodstained skin, the last hint of fire in them fades and the slate shadow is back, grim and forbidding. "You've never heard of the Marigny emerald." He speaks to Connor, but the words are for me, and they break my heart. "The ring on your sister's hand is a family heirloom that she wears to honor her mother."

He stares at me over Connor's shoulder, at the silent tears rolling down my cheeks. The grim shadow hardens into stern, cold lines. "You don't care about me one way or the other," he says flatly. "Sometimes you look in on Jeremiah at the lake house. You know me only as a relative who occasionally comes by, once every few years perhaps, no more."

I feel Jeremiah stiffen at my side. "No," he mutters, staring at Antoine. "Don't do this."

But Antoine's remorseless voice goes on, battering relentlessly at my being, tearing me apart every bit as much as it does watching him wipe Connor's memory. "You hardly even remember me at all," he says softly.

"And after tonight, you won't ever have to see me again."

CHAPTER 26

GONE

*H*ey, Tessa.

It's dusk, one week since the night in the tunnels, and I'm writing this lying on my big four-poster bed. The power has been turned on, but I still use my string of fairy lights. They make my bedroom feel magical. I need to remind myself that magic exists.

Down past the jetty, the river moves, molasses thick. Every time I look down at it, I half expect to see him leaping out of his boat, as he did that first day we met.

But Antoine is gone.

He didn't say goodbye. The last time I saw him was when he compelled Connor to forget everything that happened. He must have done the same with Avery, because when I saw her at school she mumbled something about how she hoped Connor didn't think badly of her, but nothing at all about opening a strange iron door by magic. That's not the kind of thing anyone just forgets, special cookies or not.

Jeremiah told me Antoine has gone to Oklahoma, where the descendants of the Natchez live. He's gone in search of anything that might help us ensure the binding remains closed. I haven't heard any more from Jeremiah since that conversation, the day after my wedding. Connor mentioned that he drove out to the lake house to check in on him, but that nobody answered the door. I know Jeremiah blames me for Antoine leaving. Because of me, he lost the only real family he has, while I kept mine. I miss Jeremiah almost as much as I do Antoine. Without him, there is nobody to remember with. Nobody to reassure me that I didn't simply dream Antoine himself. And everything that happened after I met him.

The only reminders of Antoine's place in my life are the ring on my left hand and the marriage certificate I found tucked beneath my pillow, the morning after what should have been our wedding night. I know he must have put it there while I slept. I dreamed of him, I think, looking down at me with his eyes rich and glowing as they'd been when he faced me in the church. I woke with tears on my cheeks and my skin still tingling with the memory of his touch, and when I found the certificate I laid there and read it over and over, as if imprinting the words on my mind could bring him back and make it all real again.

Since then, nothing.

I know why he did it. And part of me knows it was the right thing to do. Connor is happier than I've ever known him, working every spare moment on the mansion, so full of ideas and excitement he even smiles when Avery comes around—which she does, a lot. The part of me that understands his decision thinks of all the reasons it is the right thing for us both. Logical reasons, like the fact that three centuries is an impossible age gap by anyone's standards, and that breaking an ancient curse is hardly the basis for a long-term relationship. Or that the very concept of "until death do us part" is entirely ridiculous when one of us is, as Antoine said himself, already dead.

But on evenings like this when I close my eyes, I can smell the scent of summer magnolias and cedar. I can see the sunlight turn his eyes to molten gold as we stood in the church. I remember how it feels to be drawn in against him, so close I don't know where I leave off and he begins. I remember how it felt when he drank from me, as if I were falling inside him, to a place where only he and I existed, and nothing could ever harm us again. I think of the first day we met and the way he brushed my hair from my face. Then I let the memories fall thick and fast around me and try not to feel cheated at the thought that I have barely a handful of memories with a man who will live to make an eternity of them.

Downstairs I can hear Cass and Avery tumble out of Cass's car. They've come for dinner. Connor is grilling steaks on the porch, and I can hear his dry teasing and Avery's giggle, the clink of bottles. I twist the emerald ring and feel the ghost of Antoine's touch as he slipped it on my finger.

If I close my eyes, I can see him, leaning up against his old teal Chevy, his eyes like a storm-tossed sea.

Always.

The curtain in the window ripples with a rogue breeze, and on the jetty far below, for a moment I think I see a tall, lean figure, and my heart leaps. But when I look back, it's gone, just a trick of the light.

I don't know what you make of all this, Tessa. All I know is that I'm going to be writing to you a whole lot more now.

I guess that's a good thing.

Your twin,
    Harper

~

You have just read an advance copy of Red Magnolia, #1 in the Nightgarden Saga. On the following pages you will find an excerpt from the second book in the Saga, Moon Vine.

Your reviews matter more than I can say. Please add Red Magnolia to your Read list on Goodreads and leave a review here, or from September 2021 on Amazon.

I'd love to send you a hard copy for your bookstagram. Please contact me at lucyholdenparanormal@gmail.com if you are interested.

If you would like to advance read the other books in the series, links follow the excerpt on the following pages.

MOON VINE SAMPLE CHAPTERS

PROLOGUE

*H*ey, Tessa.

I CAN FEEL WINTER COMING.

The moon vine I planted winds about my window, buds stubbornly closed during the day, unfurling like a silent secret when night falls. The flowers remind me of you, pale and delicate on the outside, but with vivid shades of purple and crimson hidden at their core. Like you, they're stronger than they look. Resilient. Willing to grow here even though they don't belong. That's how I often think of you. You smiled and laughed, even though part of you must always have known you couldn't stay long. That was your hidden strength, your crimson core. I see your face every night as the petals unfold. I hear you whisper my name on the breeze that carries their scent through my window.

Sometimes I don't know what is real, anymore.

I always thought you'd be at my wedding. You weren't, though. Nobody was. It was just Antoine, me, and the priest he compelled to marry us. All I have to remind me it was real is a marriage certificate I keep hidden in a box under my bed, a bloodstained dress I can't bear to wash, and an emerald ring Connor thinks is a family heirloom. It is. Just not one from my family.

It's the famous Marigny emerald, not that anyone knows. Who'd believe me, anyway?

The dreams have stopped. Since the title to the house was changed to my married name, Harper Marigny, I don't hear Keziah whisper to me anymore. Antoine said the magic in the binding spell protects the owner of the house from her mind control. I think she's still awake, though. I can feel her, a strange current on the air, as if she's waiting for something. I guess creatures like Keziah never stop waiting.

Creatures like Antoine.

Vampires.

I know what he is. But I can't think of him in the same way as Keziah. He was created to save people from what she and Caleb are, to defeat the monsters rather than become one of them. Yet I know he believes, in some dark place inside even I can't touch, that he shares their nature. I know that's why he left.

Jeremiah came back to school before Thanksgiving. He told me that Antoine went to Oklahoma, where most of the descendants of the Natchez nation live now. He's gone in search of something that will put a final end to the deadly vampires sleeping beneath my house. I know that Jeremiah blames me for Antoine leaving. He avoids me, though he and Connor have become quite good friends. Once, in class, when Mr Corbin called me Harper Ellory, I caught Jeremiah staring at the ring on my finger. He gave me a sad smile that broke my heart.

I wish we were still friends. I wish I had someone, anyone, to talk to.

I thought I felt alone when first we came here. Since Antoine left, though, I'm alone in a different way. A hard way. Antoine isn't dead - well, he is, I guess, but he is still present in the world. He may as well be dead to me, though. I've begun to call him a hundred times, but my finger hovers over the phone, then slides away. I know he isn't coming back. I saw it in his face that night by the tunnels, when he compelled

Connor to forget everything he'd seen. When I remember the way Connor looked that night, how ready he was to walk away from the restoration grant he worked so hard to get just to keep me safe, I know it was the right thing to do. I can't be the one to take away Connor's dream, any more than he could follow it if he thought I was in danger. But I didn't know that staying here without Antoine would feel like this, as if I'm in limbo, with the only person capable of pulling me out of it as profoundly gone as if he had never been.

Connor can't know I married a vampire to save us from danger. And I'm guessing he wouldn't see it that way if he did know. So the marriage certificate stays in the box beneath the bed, and I wear a three century old emerald worth more than the house to school every day.

I know I should take it off.

But I just can't, Tessa.

Happy Thanksgiving, I guess, wherever you are.

Your twin
    Harper

Moonvine continues on the next page...

MOON VINE CHAPTER 1

"*D*id you know it's my birthday next month?" Avery is swinging her legs off the end of the dock. I'm painting. The air smells of newly turned earth from the garden I've been digging just behind us.

"It would be difficult to forget," says Cass dryly without looking up from her book. She's sitting on the wooden boards with her legs stretched out, her back against a post. "Considering you mention it on a daily basis."

"Well, it's important. I am sixteen, going on seventeen." Avery stands up as she sings the words and does an exaggerated twirl. "But unlike Liesl in *The Sound of Music*, I do *not* need somebody older and wiser telling me what to do." She turns to me. "Which is why I was hoping you'd say yes to me having my party here." She gives me her best doe-eyed, pleading look. "That way we can celebrate with no parentals. And besides, this place is awesome." Given that Avery is impossibly beautiful, even I find it difficult to say no to the wide brown eyes and tragic face. But then I imagine a mansion full of drunk, hormonal teenagers dancing right above the two starving vampires in our cellar and steel myself to refuse.

"It's not really my decision," I say, doing my best to look apologetic. "Connor isn't much of a party person, and the mansion is his project. I doubt he'll want to risk damaging anything."

"Leave Connor to me." Avery leaps to her feet and marches toward the house with more alacrity than strictly necessary.

I sigh. "Connor doesn't have a chance, does he?"

"Nope." Cass smiles at me. She has a peaceful, quiet presence and often comes down to the dock to read a book while I'm painting or gardening. When I first knew her, I thought her sense of humor was a little sharp, her one liners a touch snarky. A little time, though, has made me realise the snark is definitely more an Avery thing. Cass sometimes affects it, but this, I've learned, is more of a façade, one she adopts to protect herself, to mask her true nature. In reality she is one of the most gentle people I know. When we're alone, she lets the mask drop, and the smart comments with it. I suspect that the edgy sense of humor is down to her lifelong friendship with Avery, who at times can have a sharp tongue indeed. Cass is compassionate and kind, probably why Avery and she have remained close for so long. Underneath her exterior, Avery is deeply insecure. She needs friends like Cass who don't compete with her, who offer a gentle place to land when she screws up – which Avery definitely has an ability to do.

I normally hate people watching me work. Cass's presence, though, is soothing. And since Antoine left, I'm in no position to reject company. Sometimes I think about telling Cass everything that happened. If anyone might understand, I think it would be her. But I know I can't. Even if she didn't think I was completely insane, it isn't fair to drag anyone else into this.

"Come on." I take down my canvas and unscrew the easel. "We should go up and rescue Connor."

"Are you sure Connor wants to be rescued?" Cass shoots me a sideways look. "Avery is the kind of girl that every boy dreams about, and she's been spending every waking minute here for weeks." For a moment, I want to tell Cass that going by the way Connor looks at her when he thinks nobody is watching, it isn't Avery he's dreaming about, but I figure that would only make things weird. I say instead, "Avery isn't really Connor's type," and leave it there.

The sound of Avery's laughter trickles through the back door. She and Connor are in the kitchen. I leave my easel propped up against the wall and follow Cass through in time to hear Avery say, "But if we promise to stay out of the library, you'll say yes? Everyone will be outside, anyways. I was thinking a fire by the river and fairy lights throughout the garden." She turns to me, her eyes sparkling. "Connor's cool with it," she beams. I give Connor a questioning look over her shoulder, and he raises his hands in a gesture of half apology, half surrender.

I swallow my inner dread. "Sounds like you've got it all planned." I put on my best attempt at a smile. "How many people are you thinking?"

"That's the best part." Avery can barely contain her excitement. "Your place is huge. The police never come out this way, and you don't have any close neighbors to complain about the noise. I figure we can invite our whole class without any trouble. But it will take me time to set it all up. You're going to be seeing a lot of me in the next few weeks." The look she gives Connor is enough to sear the paint from the walls. Connor glances sideways at Cass then awkwardly down at the ground. He mumbles something about getting tools from his truck and makes a fast exit. I wince inwardly at Avery's look of disappointment as she watches him go. I suspect Avery has never had to put in a moment's effort with a man before. Connor's rejection has triggered the insecurity lying just under her carefully maintained surface. Cass is right about Avery spending every waking minute here. Barely a day goes by without her finding some excuse to come by. I love Avery, and I treasure her friendship. But I'm not entirely comfortable with the direction in which she and Connor seem headed, for either of them.

"Are you really sure you want to have your party here?" I gesture at the cracked plaster and peeling walls, the exposed wires hanging from the ceiling. "We barely have one functional bathroom, and trust me, those pipes are not at all reliable."

"And what's a party without drunk girls lining up for the bathroom? Epic love stories start that way." Avery tosses her hair and holds up a remonstrative finger. "You are not getting out of this party, Harper Ellory, no matter what you say."

I try not to wince when she says my name. Every time someone calls me by Ellory, I think of the marriage certificate hidden under my bed and feel like a fraud.

But I'm not really married, I remind myself, something I also do every time this happens. *And it isn't like I've seen my husband since our wedding day.*

That thought makes me feel inexpressibly lonely. I look up to find Cass watching me. Avery has gone back to planning where she will put people and food and is still talking as if we are listening.

"That ring you wear," Cass says quietly. "I heard you tell Avery it's a family heirloom." I nod, dropping my head so she can't see the lie in my eyes. "It's strange," she says, and I can feel her eyes on me. "I just don't remember you wearing it when you first came here. But now I never see you without it."

"I only found it again recently." I avoid her eyes.

"I haven't seen that sexy uncle of Jeremiah's around in a while." She's still watching me.

"No. I think he's left town." I summon up a bright smile. "I can't hear Avery talking, which is actually scarier than when she won't stop. Shall we go and find her?"

MOON VINE CHAPTER 2

*W*hen my phone dings the following night with a text message, I'm expecting yet another idea from Avery about her party. I see Antoine's name on the screen instead, and my heart screeches to a halt, then starts thudding again, so loud I can hear it. I stare at the name for a long time before I slide the message open. *Have found Natchez woman who knows history of seal. Her name is Noya. She will come to house to see you. Trying to find how to free you from binding. Antoine.*

Trying to find how to free you from binding.

I feel a lurch of disappointment then immediately feel stupid. Of course, he is trying to find a way around the binding. Or a way to actually kill what is sleeping in the cellar below. I knew that was what he had gone in search of. But a secret part of me wonders what it is he truly wants to free me from—the binding, or marriage to him?

I should want to be free of the marriage, I guess. It's not like getting married at seventeen is anyone's life goal.

But I don't. And it hurts more than I like to admit that Antoine seems so intent on finding a way out of it.

I twist the comforting weight of the emerald on my finger. *Always.* I remember the way he looked at me when he said that word, and how it made me feel, as if we were bound in a way nothing could ever break. Now it seems he wants nothing more than to free himself of anything that binds us together. I have a thousand unanswered questions and no way to ask them.

I wander downstairs and find Connor whistling tunelessly as he sands a wall in one of the state rooms. I take up position beside him and we work together for a while in comfortable silence. The dusk is filled with a chorus of bird call, the haunting sounds of the mourning doves that nest in the roof, the woodpeckers in the gnarled live oak beyond the window. They trill the air in such a mass of chatter it makes Connor and I look at one another and laugh. "Do you think they're talking about us?" he says.

"I doubt we're that interesting."

"You're probably right." Connor takes a pull on his beer. "I was thinking that perhaps you could paint a mural in here. On this wall. If you wanted to."

"Really?" I look at the vast expanse, already excited by what I might create. "Wouldn't that impact the restoration grant?"

"The grant covers the structure, not decoration. So long as you aren't knocking walls down, feel free to paint anything you like." He smiles. "Now, if only you looked that enthusiastic about your math homework."

"I'm never going to be excited about math homework. But this—I can't wait to get started."

"I'm glad." Connor turns back to his sanding. "You seemed like you needed something to cheer you up. You don't seem to go out much anymore." I think of the last party I went to, when Antoine compelled a pack of men from the bayou to dance naked on the road after they attacked me, and I stifle a smile. "I'm happy here." It's the truth. In reality I've never wanted to do anything other than paint and garden, anyway. I have no idea how I'm going to make a living out of either, but somehow I know I was put on this earth to do both, and so there is almost nothing in the world that could make me happier than a blank wall and paint to make it come alive and bare earth out back in which to plant.

Almost nothing.

I remember Antoine's message and turn away so Connor can't see my face. "I forgot to tell you." I strive for as casual a tone as I can manage. "I was making some enquiries at Cass's mom's shop about the supposed curse on our mansion. Selena put me in touch with a woman, Noya, from the Natchez nation up in Oklahoma. Noya apparently has an interest in alternative history. Magic, curses, that kind of thing. She's going to be in Deepwater soon and wants to come and have a look around. I said it was fine. I hope that's okay?"

"Sure thing." Connor shrugs. Then, in a studiedly casual voice to rival my own, he says, "What shop is it that Cass's mom has, again?"

My face is still hidden, so he doesn't see my smile. "It's called Witch Way. Kind of a hippy shop. But there are some really interesting artifacts and books in there and a display of old jewelry. You're such a history nerd that you'd probably like it." I wait a beat. "Cass works there in the afternoons after school to give her mom a break."

"That's nice of her." Connor is going for a neutral tone, but I can see the faint tinge of color at the neck of his T-shirt.

"Cass is a nice girl." Now I'm really stirring the pot, but I can't help it. Cass *is* a nice girl. And if anyone needs a nice girl, it's my brother. Connor is ridiculously good-looking. He's also completely unaware of it and a genuinely kind person. As a result, he's always been a magnet for girls with insecurity issues. Avery, for all her stunning good looks, is classic Connor kryptonite. He doesn't have the heart to tell her outright that he isn't interested, and the longer it goes on, the more he will find himself stuck in something he doesn't want, all because he doesn't quite have the courage to approach the girl he actually wants.

He clears his throat and takes another swallow of his beer. I take pity on him and change the subject. "How are we going to manage this party of Avery's?"

Connor shakes his head and rolls his eyes skyward as he sands. "Truly, I don't know. The place is a health and safety nightmare. I'll have to put barricades up everywhere and lock what doors we can."

"Especially the library." I try to keep my tone light, but it's been worrying me ever since Avery came up with the idea. "I think we should put a lock on that door and make sure people know it is out of bounds. If anyone accidentally opens that hidden passageway, we could find ourselves with a drunk accident on those dark stairs."

"Of course." Connor frowned. "Maybe I should go down there and take a look. You know, I'd actually forgotten about that staircase. And the cellar." Too late, I remember Antoine compelling Connor to do exactly that.

"I don't think there's any need to go that far," I say hastily. "You said it's dangerous, remember? Maybe just lock the door to keep others out." Connor nods, but there is a faint crease between his brows as if he's trying to remember something, and I curse my own stupidity. I know my brother too well. He's unlikely to forget about it again, not without Antoine there to make sure he does. And Antoine isn't here.

It always comes back to that.

"I'm working on a house close to town tomorrow. How about I drive you to school and pick you up?" Connor turns away to sand a doorframe. His voice has that same super casual note that red-flags exactly how much he doesn't want me to notice what he's actually saying. "Maybe we could go to that witch shop on the way home. There might be some things in there worth a look."

"Sure," I say, smiling to myself. "Why not?"

We sand on in companionable silence, the chorus of birdsong giving way to the lonely, distant caw of a nighthawk.

MOON VINE CHAPTER 3

*T*he next day when Connor drops me off at school, Jeremiah is talking to Avery in the parking lot. She breaks off the conversation and rushes over as soon as she spots us. Connor sighs audibly but smiles like the nice guy he is. Jeremiah's face falls as he watches Avery make a beeline for Connor, and I shoot him a sympathetic smile, but when he sees me watching him, his expression hardens and he turns away.

So, I'm still not forgiven, then.

Avery is chatting away about arrangements for the party and is pushing a reluctant Connor to make a time to meet. The sister in me really wants to mention going to Cass's shop this afternoon, just to force Connor to confront the triangle I see closing in around him, but my inner sadist proves unequal to creating such havoc. In the end, I watch with some exasperation as Connor grudgingly agrees to be home on the weekend, and Avery begins planning what she is going to bring along and what jobs need to be done. I take it from the long list that I'm likely to have a house guest all weekend. I don't mind, if I'm honest. I know Avery comes to drool over Connor, but she truly does have a beautiful heart, and I like having her around, even though I know it isn't ideal for Connor.

"I'll see you this afternoon," I mouth to Connor behind Avery's back as we head into school. He gestures frantically at the exit to the lot, and I understand he means he will meet me outside the gates. I shake my head in mock remonstration and he rolls his eyes as he pulls out in his truck. I'm still grinning when I turn to go inside and actually walk right into Jeremiah.

"Sorry," I say awkwardly. "I didn't do that on purpose." For a moment I think he's going to just ignore me, then his face softens a little, and he ducks his head. "I know." He gives me a small smile. "How are you, Harper?"

I half shrug and don't answer. "How are you?" I ask instead. "I've been out to see you a couple of times, but you're not home a lot." *Or you're not answering the door for me,* I think, but don't say.

"I've been doing some work for your brother after school and on the weekends."

"Sure. Connor mentioned you were." Actually, he hasn't, and I'm suddenly tempted to invite Avery along this afternoon just to annoy him.

"I need to talk to you." Jeremiah looks around the corridor and lowers his voice. "I heard from Antoine last night. He's sending someone down to look at the mansion." I'm about to say that he sent me the same message, but then I see the light in Jeremiah's eyes, and realize that hearing from Antoine might well be the highlight of his week. I don't want to diminish his delight, so I don't say anything except to thank him for letting me know. "I was thinking that maybe I might come over when this Noya lady does," he goes on, his eyes shifting to me then away again, as if he's not sure what I will say to that.

"I think that's a great idea," I say, trying not to show how happy I am. "Connor might appreciate some help around the place, too, if you've got spare time. We've got a lot to organize before this party of Avery's."

"Will Avery be there this weekend? Noya's related to her, you know. Some distant Natchez connection. It might be good for them to meet. And maybe I can help take some of the work for the party off

Connor's shoulders." He does an even worse job than Connor does of hiding his interest. I pretend not to notice.

"Yes, Avery's planning to stay all weekend, from what I can gather." Mentally I'm changing the Connor, Avery, and Cass triangle to a square that puts Jeremiah as close to Avery as he can get. And I can't help but wonder about the coincidence of Noya and Avery being related. Somehow I doubt it's coincidence at all. Unfortunately, only one person is likely to be able to answer that question, and he certainly won't be joining us this weekend.

"Well, I'll see you this weekend, then." Jeremiah gives me the closest thing resembling a smile that I've had from him since Antoine left. "It's good to talk to you, Harper." I watch him go, torn between happiness that we are on better terms at last, and creeping worry at the thought of the tangled emotional web growing between my brother and my friends. I try to shake it off. Being closer to the one person who knows my secrets makes me feel temporarily less alone. I'm not ready to lose Jeremiah again. I can only hope Avery lets him down gently, rather than with the careless crash I suspect her capable of.

After school I escape the lot without being accosted by Avery, and Connor pulls out immediately. I swear he's actually checking his rearview mirror. "You know," I say conversationally as he heads into town, "it would have served you right if I'd told Avery where you're going this afternoon. I can't believe you didn't tell me Jeremiah was working with you after school."

Connor lifts a shoulder. "Didn't think it mattered. Why? Do you like him? You went to a party or something with him a while back, I remember."

"Yes. But it's nothing like that. We're just friends, is all." I mentally kick myself. Secrets hold so many traps. I remember sitting by Connor's blood-soaked body with Jeremiah while we waited for Antoine to hunt down Keziah and Caleb. Connor doesn't remember any of it. He has no idea why Jeremiah would be any more than a casual acquaintance.

We pull up in front of Witch Way. Through the window I can see several figures moving around, more customers than I've ever seen at one time. "Looks kind of crowded." But Connor's eyes are fixed on Cass's tall figure behind the counter, and he's already opening the door. "Couple more won't matter any," he says, and I try not to smile.

The hanging chimes make a tune as we open the door and step inside. Cass looks up from the counter, and for a moment her face breaks into an unguarded smile, her eyes glowing softly as she looks at Connor. I feel something in my heart shift, for my brother and for Cass.

"Hey," says Connor quietly.

"Hey." Cass smiles, and even a blind man could see that there is nobody else in the room for either of them. I'm moving surreptitiously off to the side to give them some space when Cass says, "It's good timing that you came today. Noya and her nephew, Tate, have come all the way from Oklahoma to have a look at the Marigny mansion. You've just saved me a drive out to introduce them. Noya— this is Connor Ellory and his sister, Harper."

The couple at the desk turn around, and the woman, who is tall and elegant, with long dark hair, jeans, and a boho shirt, puts out her hand. "It's nice to meet you both," she says, shaking our hands and smiling. "I'm Noya, and this is my nephew, Tate. He's a specialist in the tribal history of this area." Tate is even taller than his aunt and looks about the same age as Antoine, early twenties. He's got the same sharp, angular features as Noya, as well as her long dark hair, tied back at his neck. His smile is as open as Noya's and he takes my hand with genuine interest. "Harper," he says, but he isn't looking at my face. He is staring at the ring on my hand. When he looks back up at me his smile is firmly in place, but I saw it, the moment when his mouth tightened and his eyes narrowed, and so when I answer him I can't quite hide the wariness in my tone.

"Tate." His hand is cool and smooth, but I sense strength in his brief grip. "I didn't realize two people would be coming."

"No." His smile still hasn't wavered, but something lurks behind his eyes. I can see it, and I suspect he knows I can, because there is a wry twist to his mouth when he says, "I was a late addition to the journey. I just came to keep my aunt company. We haven't seen one another in a while."

"Tate has been lecturing in Georgia for a time. It's good to have him home." Noya casts her nephew a warm smile. There is a slight sadness to her face, as if she carries grief somewhere inside. It's an expression I know well. I get the impression she is the kind of person to keep her troubles private, however.

Tate gestures to a cabinet full of jewelry, mostly beaten silver filled with stones like lapis and moonstone. Most of the cabinets are lit, but this one is dark, the pieces clearly less valuable than some of the others. At the back of the rows of silver lies another, dusty row of earrings and pendants carved from wood, bone, and shell. They are crude and clunky, not very attractive. "I notice you have some pendants carved from wood and bone," Tate says to Cass. "Where do you get them?"

"Mom does the ordering. I'm not sure."

"This one suits you." Tate holds up a shell piece with a spiral design. He's right, it does look beautiful next to Cass's skin, and she is clearly a little flustered by the attention and his warm smile. Connor frowns. As if sensing his tension, Tate turns the same warm smile to him. "I saw the proposal you drew for the Marigny mansion." He says the one thing guaranteed to charm my brother, and sure enough, Connor's face immediately relaxes into a self-conscious smile. "It's wonderful," says Tate, with such obvious sincerity that even my own initial reserve is rapidly fading. "I lecture in history at the University of Georgia. I'm good friends with one of the members of the Legacy Committee who decided to award you the grant. I know how excited everyone is about your plans. I can't wait to see what you've done." He and Connor instantly fall into a complex discussion about foundations and architecture, of which I understand almost nothing. I'm willing to bet Cass doesn't, either, but her eyes glow as she watches Connor talking animatedly about the mansion, and when he looks up to find her watching him, my brother smiles crookedly and looks so happy that when Tate finally turns to me, I'm all but ready to hug him.

Tate has somehow managed to draw Cass into his conversation with Connor by the jewelry cabinet and then extricates himself just as deftly. Connor is actually laughing and talking openly in a way he rarely does with anyone, and Cass seems genuinely fascinated as he tells her about his plans for the mansion. Tate and Noya join me beside the door. "It's probably a good time for us to leave," Tate says, winking at me conspiratorially.

"I met Avery and her parents earlier when we arrived in town," says Noya, quietly enough that my brother can't hear. "Avery mentioned she's heading out to see you this weekend. I thought that might be a good time to look at the mansion, if it suits you? I'd like to spend some time with Avery, too. And Jeremiah, of course. Antoine told me a lot about him."

"That sounds good." I smile at them both, fighting the fierce desire to ask what else Antoine might have said. "I'm glad you got in touch with Jeremiah," I say instead, forcing a cheerful smile. "I think it's important for him to keep a connection to the mansion."

"I imagine he's fascinated by your brother's progress," says Tate. "I gather the mansion was quite the ruin before your brother began the restoration. Jeremiah is fortunate there are grants available—mansions such as those are an expensive business to restore."

I wonder for a moment why he thinks the restoration of the mansion will benefit Jeremiah, but I don't think on it for long. There is something both warm and non-threatening about Tate. I find his presence oddly comforting, like the scent of baked bread in a house.

"I don't think his parents created much of a home," I say, smiling at Tate. "Now he's doing really well in school, and he seems to like working with Connor." What I really mean is that the sale of the mansion brought Antoine into Jeremiah's life, a trade I suspect Jeremiah would make again in a heartbeat. I catch the thought before it goes down the inevitable road straight to my heart. "My brother buying the mansion might actually be the best thing that ever happened to Jeremiah."

For the briefest moment, Tate's eyes narrow, and the warm smile falters. It's fleeting, just as it was earlier when he noticed the ring on my finger, but it's there, nonetheless.

"I didn't realize your brother actually bought the mansion," he says slowly. Is it my imagination, or is he looking at me more closely than he did before?

"Yes, we own it." I watch him carefully, but when he nods, he seems entirely unconcerned, and I think I must have imagined his reaction. I sigh inwardly.

That's the problem with secrets, I think later, as Connor and I drive home in companionable silence. *Keeping them makes you think everyone else is doing the same.*

"So Cass is going to come out this weekend, too," says Connor, as we pull up in front of the house.

He casts me a sideways glance. I manage to keep a straight face while he's looking at me, but I can't help smiling as I get out of the car.

If I can't have my own romance, I think, at least I can live vicariously through my brother's.

BUY MOON VINE TO KEEP READING, AND TURN OVER FOR MORE.

ABOUT THE AUTHOR

If you enjoyed reading Red Magnolia, please consider leaving a review on Goodreads or Amazon. Reviews help indie authors more than you can imagine - I can't tell you how much I appreciate them.

If you would like to be the first to read an advance copy of Moon Vine, or the other books in the Nightgarden Saga, please sign up here. To buy any of the books in the series, please go to Amazon.

Lucy Holden is a pseudonym for Paula Constant, an Australian author who lives in the gorgeous north western pearling town of Broome. She adores gin martinis, dreaming on the beach beneath a full moon, and having pool book club with awesome friends. The name Lucy is taken from the girl who stepped through the wardrobe in the Narnia books, and Holden refers to Paula's beloved first car.

Paula is the author of historical fiction series the Visigoths of Spain, and travel memoirs Slow Journey South and Sahara.

www.paulaconstant.com